Wild Dunedin

Enjoying the Natural History of
New Zealand's Wildlife Capital

Neville Peat & Brian Patrick

University of Otago Press

CONTENTS

1 Natural Heart of a City *5*
2 The Underlying Story *11*
3 Otago Peninsula *23*
4 Islands *49*
5 Estuaries, Inlets and Lagoons *59*
6 Forests *71*
7 Uplands *83*
8 The Taieri *99*
9 Range Roving *111*
10 Caretaking *129*
   Bibliography *136*
   Index *139*
   Acknowledgements *144*

Above: *Subalpine vegetation on the flanks of Swampy Summit overlooking the city centre. Prominent plants are Three-finger* Pseudopanax colensoi, *Inaka and Manuka.*

Published by University of Otago Press
56 Union Street West, Dunedin, New Zealand
Fax: 64 3 479 8385. Email: university.press@stonebow.otago.ac.nz

© Neville Peat & Brian Patrick 1995, 2002
First published 1995. New edition 2002. ISBN 1 877276 41 3
Cover photographs by Neville Peat
(front cover photograph from *Coasting: The Sea Lion and the Lark*, Longacre, 2001).
Illustrations by Chris Gaskin; Index by Linda Pears; Maps by Peter Scott.
Printed through Condor Production Ltd, Hong Kong

PREFACE

Welcome to the natural wonders of the Dunedin region, which spreads from the ocean to the inland ranges. As the map on the next page shows, Metropolitan Dunedin, the city proper together with its suburbs, is but a relatively small part of the total area.

This book is a comprehensive introduction to the landforms, plants and animal life of a city that professes to be the wildlife and nature heritage capital of New Zealand, a city with more than its fair share of rare and special elements. Rather than blandly list and illustrate every species of the flora and fauna native to Dunedin, we have selected the characteristic elements. Some of them will be well known to local people and to visitors. Some are less obvious; some will be revelations. We have strived for balance. In this sort of work, invertebrate fauna is too often overlooked in favour of birds and the larger animals, and yet the invertebrate world is abundant, fascinating and full of zany forms and zany behaviour.

For the most part only native species are described, and we give special emphasis to those species that are endemic to the Dunedin area. Clearly, introduced species have had an impact on the natural environment (viz. Old Man's Beard and possums) and we mention the most significant of them.

Following a chapter on the geology of Dunedin – which will intrigue Dunedin people who thought they had the measure of where they lived! – the book describes things biological from the coast westwards. The chapter breakdown is geographically/ecologically defined, but nature does not recognise human boundaries nor does it readily compartmentalise its offspring, so some species appear in more than one chapter.

The scientific expression, 'type locality', appears in the book. Taxonomists use the expression in their descriptions of plant or animal species. It pinpoints the place where a particular species was collected from and described, and where it might typically be found. The 'type specimen' or 'type population' will have come from such a place, providing a benchmark for comparing similar species.

Besides the natural history content, the book contains discussions on the conservation status of certain species – not to mention landscapes and habitats – that are rare, threatened or endangered, and some thoughts on what actions should be taken. The final chapter expands on this theme. For in the end, we must do more than simply record the elements of Dunedin that make it such a special place naturally. We want those elements to have a future.

NEVILLE PEAT AND BRIAN PATRICK

The text is strewn with scientific names as well as common and, where known, Maori names. The widespread use of scientific names is intended to be educational.

Every described life form has a species name and a genus name, and sometimes a third name that identifies a subspecies or variety. Many if not most people have three names (sometimes more), and their generic one is that which we call a surname. For fauna and flora, the genus name is expressed first.

However difficult some of the names may look, just remember that a little Greek or Latin goes a long way. If you have mastered such names as Hippopotamus, Rhododendron, Rhinoceros, Geranium, Radiata and Macrocarpa, why not extend your scientific vocabulary? Here is your chance.

The publishers acknowledge the generous support of the Dunedin Branch of the Royal Forest and Bird Protection Society of New Zealand Inc. in the publication of this book.

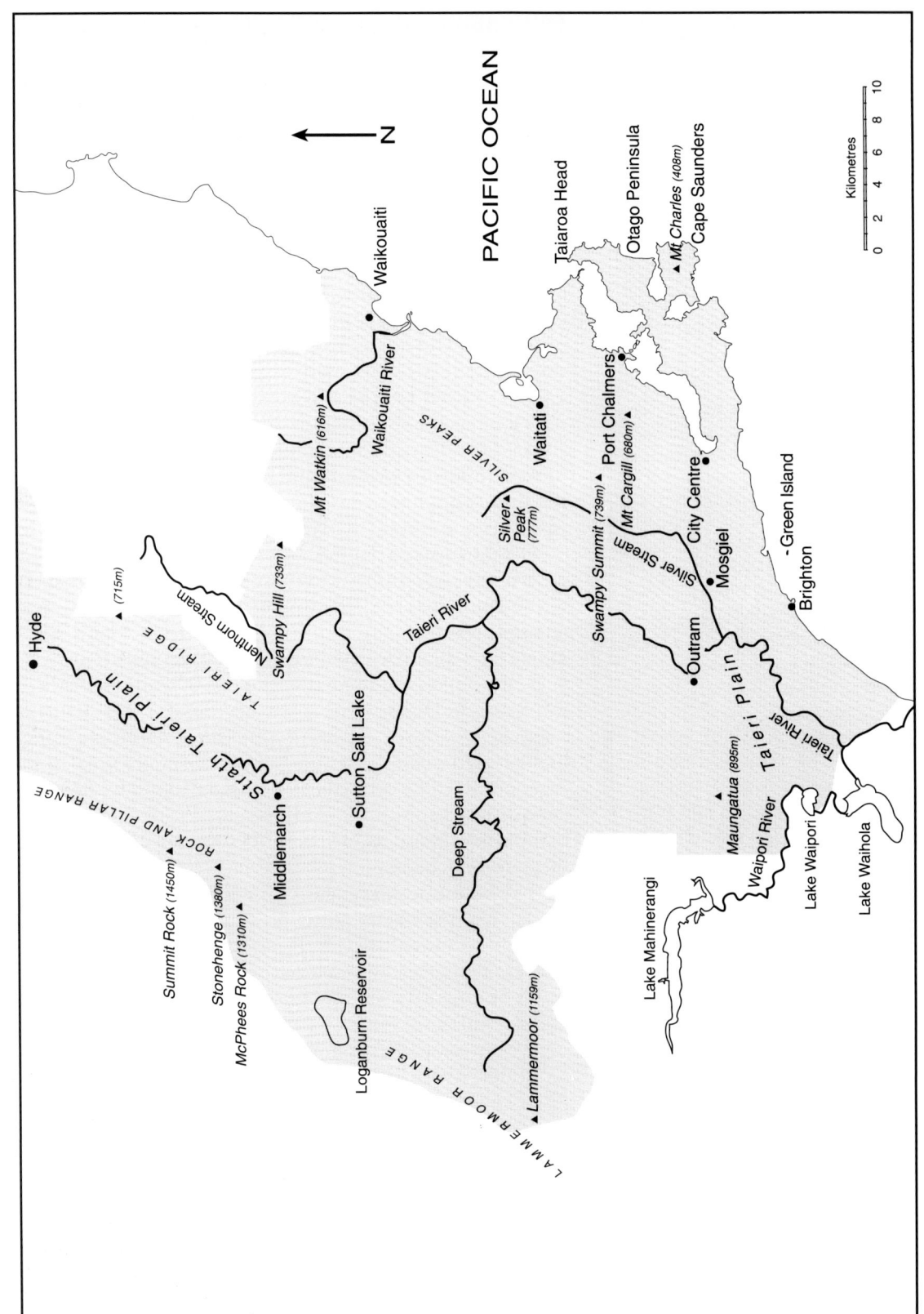

Chapter 1   NATURAL HEART OF A CITY

There are few cities on earth that are as well endowed naturally as the City of Dunedin. One reason for this is its far-flung extent. It is a city that embraces large areas of farmland, lonely hills, upland plateaux, rugged river gorges and, yes, even an alpine zone – all this for a human population of just 118,000. It takes nearly two hours to drive from the city centre – the Octagon and its avenue of elegant plane trees – to the city's treeless, tussock-clad western boundary on the Old Dunstan Road.

Dunedin, all up, encompasses 3,350 square kilometres – just over 10 per cent of the area of Otago. So it is big, but why so big? The answer lies in the reorganisation of local government in 1989, when metropolitan Dunedin spread out to embrace several boroughs and the Taieri and Silver Peaks County Council areas. The old counties contained the city's most important catchments for water supply, in particular the Deep Stream catchment which has its origins in the Lammermoor Range. Thus water supply has had a major part to play in enlarging the city boundaries as far as mountain ranges to the west. These ranges form the eastern margin of Central Otago.

Of course, big does not necessarily mean better when it comes to natural history or anything else. But chances are that biological diversity (biodiversity) will increase in proportion to area, especially if, as in Dunedin's case, the area takes in a variety of rock types, landforms, waterways, altitudes and climates.

Dunedin's climate overall is temperate, with rainfall generally adequate across the bulk of the city area and measuring 785mm on average a year in the city centre, with somewhat more rain falling in the hill suburbs. Mean temperature is 11 degrees Celsius. At the coast, temperatures are

Above: *Kowhai flowers emblazon the cliffs above Leith Valley.*

Left: *Map of Dunedin City, showing boundaries and physical features.*

Right: *City limits. Boundary fence on the summit crest of the Rock and Pillar Range, 1400m above sea level.*

Natural Heart of a City   5

Left: *Adapting to the elements – a wind-shorn Kanuka tree at Sandymount, Otago Peninsula*

moderated by the sea; inland, summers are hotter and drier than at the coast and winters bring more frosts and snow.

Onshore winds from the north-east quarter are often persistent, banking clouds on the Mt Cargill/Swampy Summit skyline and churning up harbour waters. But the most feared winds are from the south or south-west. These are the gales that cultivate wind-shear in exposed vegetation. A southerly front, approaching fast, can darken the sky in minutes and cause the air temperature to plummet by more than 10 degrees. The changeable nature of Dunedin's weather does have aesthetic compensations, though – the city is a spectacular place for cloud formations and variable lighting.

Weather is not the only changeable factor. Nothing in nature is fixed forever. There are shifts in vegetation patterns going on in many places around Dunedin. Examples are the slow, successional, uphill movement of shrubland on Flagstaff, and the wholesale takeover of the Green Island shrubland by Taupata *Coprosma repens* following the die-back of *Hebe elliptica* through, apparently, drought in the 1950s. Some changes are induced by burning off (after which native Hard tussock may overtake more palatable native grasses) or mass application of fertiliser, which can cause widespread regeneration of Matagouri in upland tussock grasslands. The Matagouri also responds to phosphate fertiliser by growing abnormally large.

Just as the plant life adjusts to changing conditions, fauna can make adjustments, too. Some moths and butterflies have adopted introduced plant species as hosts for their larvae. Red admiral butterflies, for example, have taken a shine to introduced nettles. The New Zealand falcon has probably extended its range thanks to an increase in prey species provided by introduced passerine birds. Fur seals and sea lions, virtually extinct on the mainland in the nineteenth century and for much of the twentieth century, are restaking claims on the rocky shores and beaches of Otago Peninsula.

Dunedin is best known for its Royal albatross and Yellow-eyed penguin, which have achieved icon status nationally – even internationally. But surprises are in store for anyone who cares to look beyond these icons in the fauna. Take the Royal spoonbill at Green Island, for example, or the South Island robin in the Flagstaff forest, South Island fernbird at the Waipori/Waihola wetlands, velvety Peripatus crawling about Caversham Valley bush, Clapping cicada in the Taieri Gorge, the Aoraia moth navigating through forest at night, and mountain weta confined to the harsh alpine zone of the Rock and Pillar Range, dependent on antifreeze in their blood to keep it from seizing up.

The diverse and pulsating parade of wildlife knows no bounds. It is joined from time to time by new players, occasionally vagrant birds or insects far from their known range. Moreover, ongoing research is making discoveries of new species of insects at a startling rate. Since 1980, more than

Below: *Aramoana, at the entrance of Otago Harbour, abounds in natural features – a large saltmarsh backed by salt meadow, parallel dune ridges and dune slacks, and impressive volcanic cliffs. In the distance are the hills of Otago Peninsula, including Mount Charles (408m), the highest point.*

Neville Peat

31 Dunedin species have been named. Many more have been discovered but await formal description and naming. Likewise, new records for existing plants are liable to show up – and sometimes even new species come to light.

Dunedin lays claim to 31 plants and animals that are endemic (see box). Nowhere else on earth do they occur. It is a list that will no doubt be added to as time goes by. The city is a centre of biodiversity.

Because of its size and its range of habitats – from beaches of shining sand to frozen patterned ground in the alpine zone – Dunedin has more natural nooks left to be explored in depth than any New Zealand city. Moreover, it is much easier to find an alpine experience in Dunedin compared to North Island cities because the alpine zone is several hundred metres lower.

Although climate is important in determining the range of habitats and species present, a more fundamental factor is the tectonic history, which gives rise to the rocks in the first place, and the age and lie of the land surfaces. So it is to geology we turn first.

Above: *One of Dunedin's three endemic caddis,* Olinga fumosa, *which is a diurnal (daylight active) species found in streams on the slopes of Swampy Summit. The smooth horn-shaped larval cases are attached to rocks in streams at mid-altitude.*

Below: *View of Lower Taieri Plain from the subalpine shrubland/grassland zone of Maungatua.*

DUNEDIN ENDEMICS

Plants (5) — Locality
- *Helichrysum intermedium* var. *tumidum* — Otago Peninsula
- *Myosotis* new species — Strath Taieri\Lammermoor Range
- *Celmisia haastii* var. *tomentosa* — Rock and Pillar Range
- *Abrotanella patearoa* — Rock and Pillar Range
- *Kelleria villosa* var. *barbata* — Rock and Pillar Range

Fish (2)
- *Galaxias eldoni* — Lower Taieri catchment
- *Galaxias pullus* — Lower Taieri catchment

Moths (10)
- *Gymnobathra* new species — Lammermoor Range
- *Glyphipterix* new species — Lammermoor Range
- *Gelophaula* new species — Rock and Pillar Range
- *Kiwaia* new species — Rock and Pillar Range
- *Tortricidae* new genus and new species (3) — Rock and Pillar Range
- *Eudonia* new species — Otago Peninsula
- *Ichneutica* new species — Rock and Pillar Range
- *Meterana* new species — Rock and Pillar Range

Caddis (3)
- *Olinga fumosa* — Swampy Summit area
- *Pseudoeconesus paludis* — Swampy Summit area/Otago Peninsula
- *Oeconesus angustus* — Lee Stream area

Crane-fly (1)
- *Zelandotipula* new species — Dunedin forests

Beetles (6)
- *Prodontria montis* — Rock and Pillar/Lammermoor Range
- *Oopterus* new species — Lammermoor Range
- *Allocharis* new species — Lammermoor Range
- *Irenimus similis* — Lammermoor Range
- *Irenimus patricki* — Lammermoor Range
- *Irenimus dugdalei* — Lammermoor Range

Snails (1)
- *Alsolemia cresswelli* — Dunedin forests

Harvestmen (2)
- *Nuncia sublaevis* — Dunedin forests
- *Prasma sorenseni regalia* — Coastal Dunedin

Peripatus (2)
- New genus and species (2) — Dunedin forests (Caversham/Leith Valley)

Ancient marine life was otherworldly and is nowhere to be seen today, except as fossils

Bottom to top: A long-snouted whale ancestor or Archaeocete; a turtle, similar to a Leatherback, that roamed the Otago coast, and a large long-billed penguin that lived 30 million years ago.

Chris Gaskin

Chapter 2 **THE UNDERLYING STORY A rock concert**

> Was Dunedin a tropical paradise once upon a time?
> In rocks just north of Dunedin, dating back more than 20 million years, there is fossil evidence of coconut palms.

If rocks could resonate, the land lying between the Rock and Pillar Range and the coast would produce a curious medley, for it is a land built of widely varying rock types, some ancient and slow to form, some born in a molten rush.

Can you hear the humming? Listen out for country-and-western tunes from schist outcrops inland, and sea shanties from coastal sandstone and other sedimentary rocks of marine origin. As for volcanic rocks like basalt, stand by for some heavy-metal, hard and explosive.

Neville Peat

Rock art: As basalt in a lava flow cools, distinctive jointed columns are sometimes formed – as uniformly shaped and close-fitting as any Inca stonemason could have fashioned. This exposure of jointed column-forming basalt is at Black Head, on the coast just south of St Clair.

Overseas and in Dunedin, outcrops of columnar basalt have become tourist attractions – Dunedin's Organ Pipes on the slopes of Mt Cargill are especially well known. There are also spectacular outcrops at Lovers' Leap and the Pyramids on Otago Peninsula, and at Black Head (right), where the rock columns meet the sea. A protective covenant negotiated by the Department of Conservation with the company quarrying the basalt at Black Head covers the outer end of the headland. Safe public access to the outermost rock features is planned.

The result of this diversity in rock types is an offbeat ensemble of landscapes and geological features.

The schist has the oldest ancestry, dating back some 200 million years. Its story begins on the seabed, with the gradual accumulation of sand and silt to form sandstone and siltstone kilometres deep. Over eons, compressed and heated, these rocks were transformed to schist, then slowly uplifted. Schist underlies everything – the layers of sedimentary rocks that came later and the relatively recent volcanic ones. The hills and ranges away from the coast are built of schist. It also extends seaward, a platform for the continental shelf adjacent to the coast.

Strange as it may seem, mountain ranges like Maungatua and Rock and Pillar are relatively new features on the landscape. Seventy million years ago the Dunedin region was very different. It was a peneplain of schist – fairly flat and lying close to sea level. The sea invaded this landscape; at times it was deep, at times shallow, and it left its mark in the form of sediments and fossils, layer upon distinctive layer, including limestone. Before and after this flooding by the sea, river gravels and swampy deposits added terrestrial imprints.

Left, bottom to top: the rocks are schist in the seabed (the oldest rocks), sandstone (marine sediments, about 20 million years old), basalt columns (about 11 million years) and schist again as alpine tors.

Ocean bedrock to range-top tors – 200 million years of geological history

The Underlying Story 11

About 13 million years ago, the coast convulsed with volcanic activity. Vents opened, there were ash showers, and red-hot lava flowed. The first eruptions were probably seated under the sea. This was no single cataclysmic event but rather a drawn-out process of sporadic eruptions and repeated flows – a 'shield volcano', built up over three million years. At Aramoana, no fewer than 25 flows have been identified in the cliff profiles. The volcano grew to be an imposing knuckle attached to the coast, perhaps reaching about 1,000m at its peak – higher than the Maungatua Range (895m) and well above the present-day height of Mt Cargill (680m).

In the 10 million years since the volcanism transformed the coastal landscape and scattered volcanic features across the hinterland as far as the Maniototo, the forces of erosion have substantially reduced the hard core of the volcano. Port Chalmers, Portobello Peninsula and the mid-harbour islands mark its centre. A rift developed though the middle of the volcano that followed a line of weakness or faulting in the Earth's crust. When sea levels rose and the sea invaded this 'valley', Otago Peninsula became an island. Today it is reconnected to the mainland by a tombolo – the sandy flats of Tainui, St Kilda and South Dunedin. Otago Harbour and the city metropolitan area occupy the deeply-eroded remnants of the volcano: witness the steep-

Above: *Caversham sandstone is strikingly exposed on the 30m-high cliffs near Tunnel Beach, between St Clair and Black Head. The sandstone is fossil-rich, containing evidence of ancient marine life, including sharks and shellfish. On this section of coast a low, flat promontory protects Tunnel Beach, the destination of one of Dunedin's most popular walking tracks.*

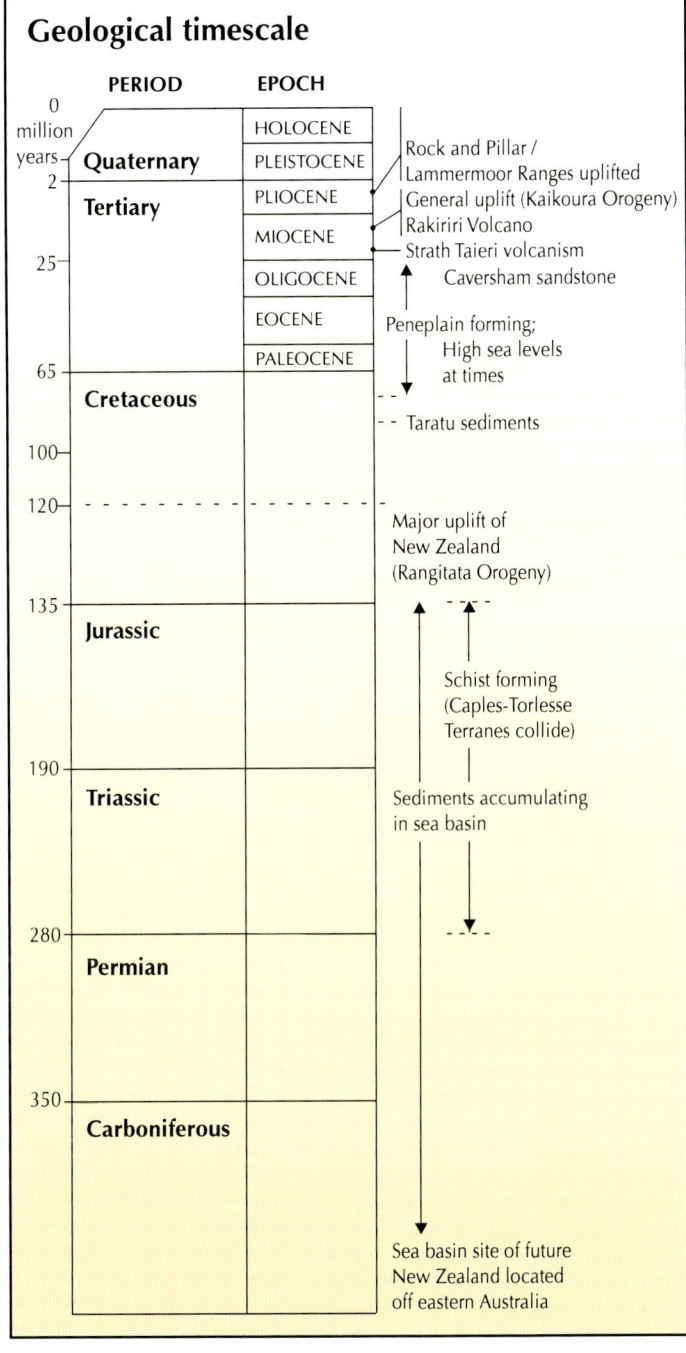

Left: *Echo from the Eocene.* Unlike any existing forms of penguin, this large long-billed specimen inhabited the Otago coast some 40 million years ago, when sea levels were higher. Its skull and bill, preserved in fine-grained mudstone, were recovered from Burnside cement works quarry. Of all the fossil penguins found in the southern hemisphere, the Burnside penguin is remarkable for the intact condition of its skull. It has yet to be formally described.

ness of the arterial routes leading from the city centre – Caversham Valley Road, Stuart Street Extension and the Northern Motorway.

Volcanic rocks, chiefly dark-grey basalt, overlie older sedimentary rocks such as Caversham Sandstone, Concord Greensand and Abbotsford Mudstone. There is a good example of this in Frasers Gully. In turn, the volcanic rocks are covered by a consolidated mantle of wind-blown silt and dust, called loess, which blew in from the Central and Western regions of Otago, and also from the riverbeds and estuaries east of Dunedin, at times when the continental shelf was exposed by lower sea levels. Around Dunedin the loess is often 1m deep. This lowering of sea levels occurred during the ice ages of the last five million years, when much of the world's water was locked up as ice caps and glaciers. Around Dunedin, the coast extended a long way east, and rivers cut gorges across the continental shelf.

Human timescale is but a blink in geological terms. The hills may look immobile today but nothing is fixed. Implying movement, fault lines criss-cross the landscape, notably the Akatore Fault south of Taieri Mouth and the Titiri and Maungatua Faults of the Taieri area. The hills and ranges beyond the volcano to the west are relatively young, pushed up only in the last three million years. And they are still growing. Still humming.

Fiery Origins

The same view, 12 million years apart. The photo shows Otago Peninsula, Otago Harbour and the backdrop of volcanic peaks today – a view from sea, with Rerewahine Point in the foreground and Taiaroa Head (Pukekura), The Mole, Aramoana and the harbour entrance at right. Papanui Inlet is partly visible at left. Saddle Hill is the peak in the middle distance. The skyline in the distance above Aramoana is formed by the Silver Peaks.

In the painting below, an eruption on the summit of Rakiriri, Dunedin's sprawling shield volcano, sends a cloud of ash seaward in its second eruptive phase about 12 million years ago. Fresh lava flows have cut swathes through the forest and shrubland that grew up in quieter periods. Cones, domes and lava flows built up the volcano over three million years. Centred on the Port Chalmers area, it attained a height of about 1,000 metres above sea level.

This portrayal is a view from sea looking south-west. Because of erosion, only a few features are recognisable today, but it is helpful to compare the painting with the photo above. The circular vent in the foreground, one of numerous vents that formed on the flanks of the volcano, represents the Rerewahine Point area adjacent to Penguin Beach at the outer end of Otago Peninsula. The ridge stretching south-west represents the backbone of Otago Peninsula. Old, eroded phonolite lava domes, from which lava flowed to the sea, are slowly being covered in vegetation. The nearer ones now form the Kaika Hill area, just north of Victory Beach. Beyond are the domes of the Highcliff area. To the right of the ridge is a depression that eroded to become Otago Harbour. The active cones, one of which is spewing ash, mark the high ground of Mt Cargill and Mihiwaka. In the distance (left, centre) is volcanic Saddle Hill and below it an inlet. The hinterland is largely flat and well vegetated.

The first eruptions 13 million years ago built up a cone from below sea level. The second eruptive phase 12 million years ago spread ash and lava east, across what would become Otago Peninsula, and as far as Wingatui and Waitati. The final eruptive phase began about 11 million years ago, building the highest hills where the Mt Cargill group now stand.

> **Rakiriri**, the ancient Dunedin volcano. The name derives from **Rangiriri** or Goat Island in Otago Harbour, which is more or less the centre of the volcano. Rakiriri is southern dialect and means literally 'angry sky'. The name is used with the permission of Otakou Maori.

Lloyd Homer/Institute of Geological and Nuclear Sciences

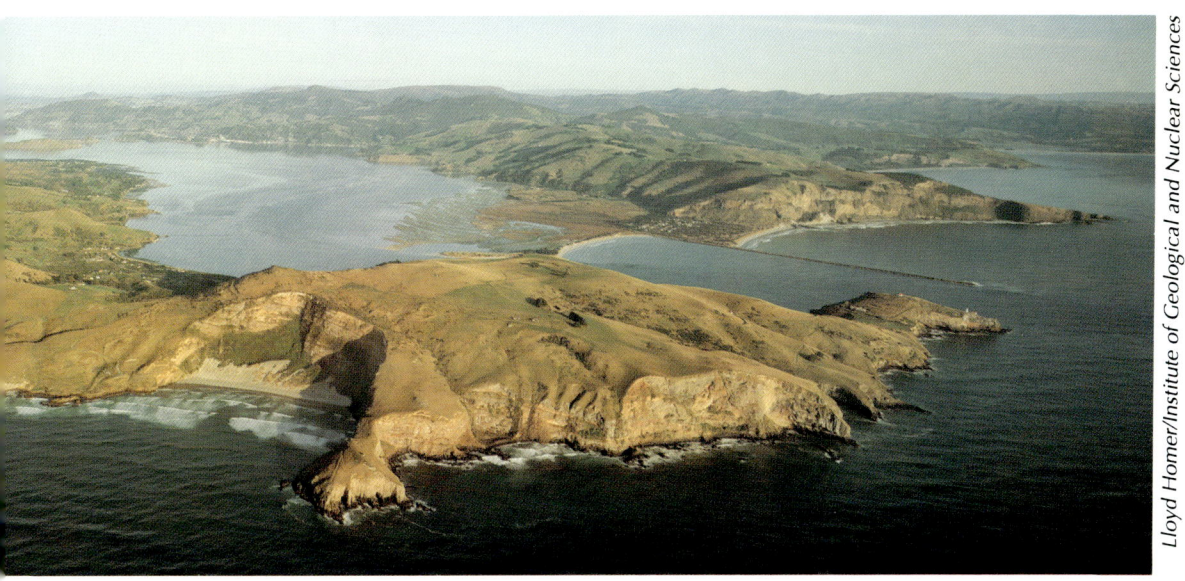

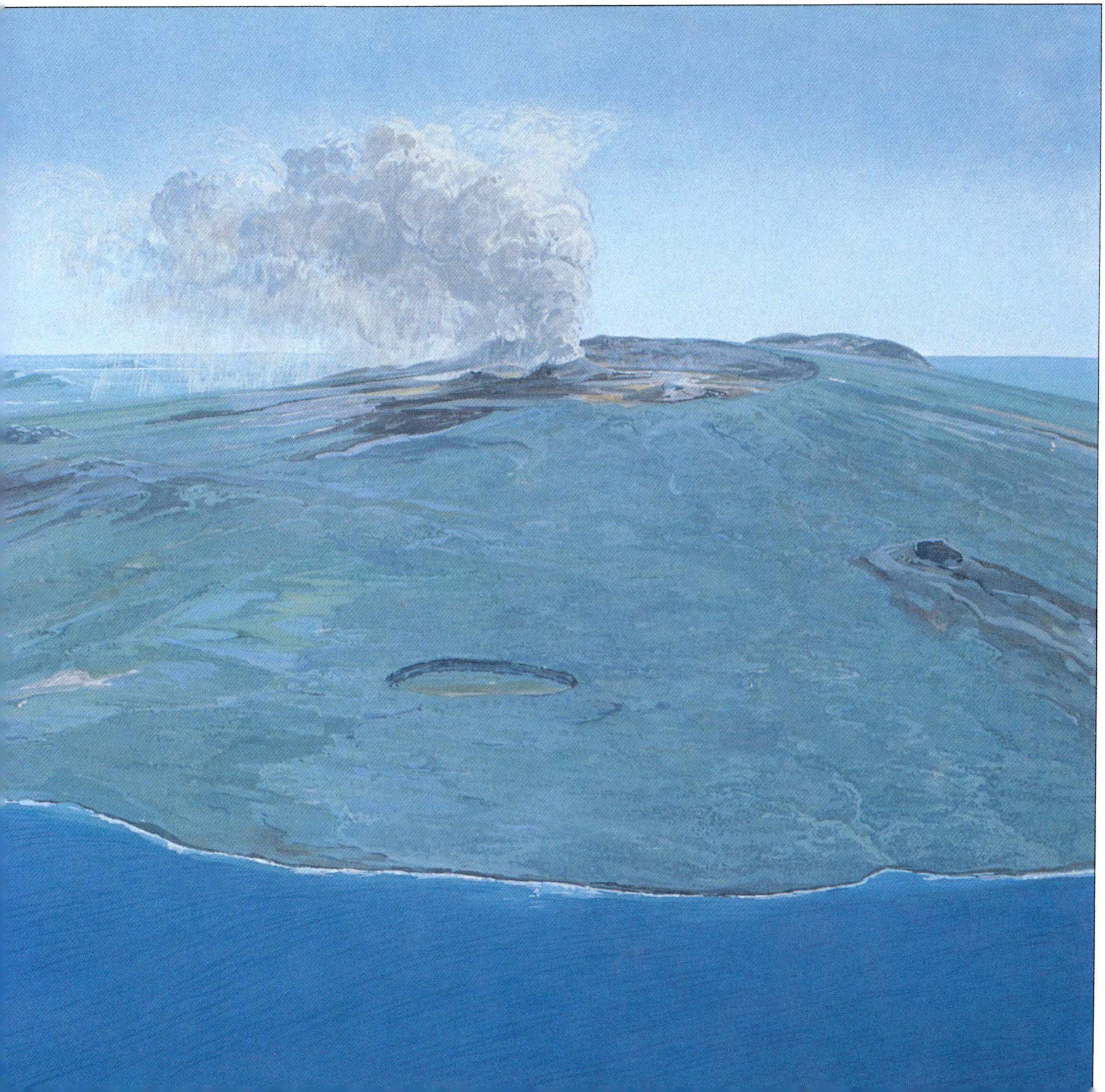

Chris Gaskin

Neville Peat

Left: *At Taiaroa Head, the tip of Otago Peninsula, there is a colourful display of volcanic rocks – a layer of dark-grey basalt overlying a layer of reddish ash and volcanic rubble. The old Maori name for the headland is Pukekura, meaning red hill.*

Right: *An artist's impression of the lake in Frasers Gully (off Kaikorai Valley), ten million years ago.*

Earth's Turn

A 10ha patch of hill country above North Taieri has a unique place in Otago's network of reserves: it is protected for its soil profile – a yellow-grey earth that has developed in loess (wind-blown silt).

Most yellow-grey earths have been modified by agriculture through drainage, cultivation, applications of fertiliser and pasture development or through forestry development. The Waiora patch, although grazed in the past, is largely unmodified and close to the altitude limit for this soil. Otago and Southland once had over 400,000ha of yellow-grey earths under forest or tussock vegetation.

The Waiora remnant is a benchmark for environmental impact studies. Under protection, the vegetation is expected to revert to manuka, then to broadleaved trees and finally a podocarp forest featuring totara and matai.

Yellow-grey earth development reflects the cold, dry climate of the last period of glaciation as well as the change to warmer, wetter conditions 10,000 years ago, when the land emerged from an ice age.

A Subtropical Touch

Ten million years ago, in the vicinity of what is now Frasers Gully (off Kaikorai Valley), a freshwater lake formed on the south-west flanks of the Dunedin volcano. During quiet periods between eruptions, where the land had cooled, dense forest grew up around the lakeshore and spread across the lower slopes of the volcano. Galaxiid fish and small aquatic animals colonised the lake.

The climate was warmer then, nurturing a forest community reminiscent of the rainforests of modern New Caledonia or Irian Jaya. Sheoaks (*Casuarina*) and large-leaved southern beech (*Nothofagus*) dominated the canopy. Trees in the protea family and large-leaved coprosmas added a subtropical touch. Leaves falling into the still waters of the lake were preserved in the sediments formed from the silica remains of millions of microscopic algae called diatoms.

The fossil leaves and pollens contained in the Frasers Gully diatomite portray a forest strikingly different from the temperate one that exists today at mid latitudes (Dunedin lies in latitude 46 degrees south). In 10 million years, the forest flora of Dunedin has undergone wholesale change. Of 23 species discovered so far, only the beech has an existing close relative – silver beech *Nothofagus menziesii*. This ancient forest flourished at quiet intervals in the three million years of volcanic activity.

> There is no evidence volcanic activity will ever revisit Dunedin. The volcano is considered extinct. This is because the Dunedin area is no longer positioned over a 'hot spot', having been rafted away from the danger by movement of the Pacific Plate, a huge segment of the Earth's crust that is grinding slowly westward.

Chris Gaskin

Ewan Fordyce

Fossil Galaxiid fish (left), and fossil leaves from Frasers Gully, Kaikorai Valley.

The Underlying Story 17

Schist – Bones of the earth

Beyond the volcanic core centred on metropolitan Dunedin and Otago Harbour is a landscape shot through with schist.

Near the coast the schist is shy, exposing itself sparingly, as on the tidal benches and low cliffs between Brighton and Taieri Mouth. Inland, however, schist makes a bold statement on the landscape, especially in the Strath Taieri and through the Taieri Gorge.

In districts such as Sutton and Nenthorn, the schist outcrops or tors evoke a strong sense of Central Otago. Where they line up as ridges protruding through the loess, the weathered outcrops resemble the ribs of some long-dead colossus, partly exhumed.

Schist is metamorphic rock, altered by heat and pressure deep in the Earth's crust. Otago's schist results from the collision of two large blocks or terranes of parent mudstone and sandstone 150 to 200 million years ago. The Torlesse terrane from the north collided with the southern Caples terrane. The rocks in the middle were buried, squeezed and folded at depths of about 15km, and heated to temperatures of 400 deg C. The resultant schist was later, and very slowly, lifted to the surface before being worn down by erosion to a nearly flat plain (peneplain). Between 30 and 70 million years ago, when sea levels were high and a shallow sea covered East Otago as far inland as the Maniototo, much of New Zealand was also under water. New Zealand was an archipelago whose largest islands were probably in the south, formed from Otago schist and Fiordland granites. In more recent geological times, an uplift in the landscape has excluded incursions by the sea.

Schist (derived from a Greek word meaning to split) is a layered rock that is prone to splitting and flaking. Wind, heat and ice all contribute to its slow decay. The quartz veins in schist, some of which are gold-bearing, offer resistance to weathering.

♦ The complexity of Dunedin's geology has benefited commercial quarrying and mining companies down the generations. Among the resources exploited: sand, gravel, diatomite, lignite (brown coal), limestone, bluestone, basalt and gold.

♦ At Ocean Grove, Scroggs Hill and Allanton there are limestone deposits up to 10m thick, overlying coal seams. Limestone also outcrops at Sandymount on Otago Peninsula and Dowling Bay on Otago Harbour, where it is mixed with layers of ash that suggest that volcanic activity started while the limestone was being formed under the sea. Limestone comprises marine sediments, animal remains (fish, shells, etc.), and sometimes plant material in a cement of calcium carbonate.

♦ The much-admired creamy sand on Dunedin's beaches has come a long way. It is derived from the weathered schist of Central Otago. Over time, it was transported down the Clutha River to the sea, then north along the coast by an ocean current – a process that continues today, although with much smaller volumes because of the hydro-electric dams on the river.

Neville Peat

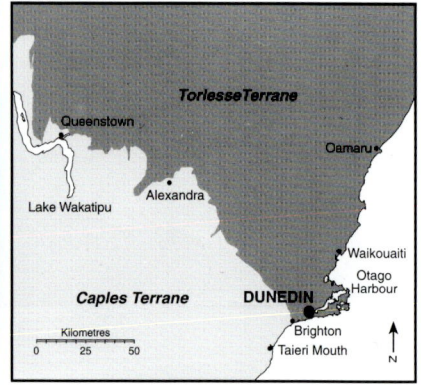

Above: *A schist outcrop or tor on the Rock and Pillar Range.*

Left: *Collision zone between the Torlesse and Caples terranes that formed Otago schist. From where it meets the sea at Brighton (see photo), the collision zone tracks inland to Alexandra, then on around the Wakatipu Basin to Mount Aspiring National Park.*

The tors (upright schist outcrops) on the summit ridge of the Rock and Pillar Range overlooking the Strath Taieri are among the most impressive in Central Otago. Reaching 1,450m at Summit Rock, the range is typical of the mountain formations of Central Otago, with a steep eastern face and a broad gently sloping western side.

Rock and Pillar, Taieri Ridge, Billy's Ridge and other ranges to the west line up in parallel (north-east trending) formation across Otago. They resemble pressure waves from the collision of two great plates of the earth's crust. This collision, traced at the surface by the Alpine Fault on the western side of the Southern Alps, has crumpled and folded the surface of Central Otago, which lies to the east of the fault, on the Pacific Plate. The result is a ripple effect on a gigantic scale. Range and basin alternate, with the location and alignment of each successive range influenced by a deep-seated fault.

These ranges are considered to be less than three million years old – some two million years younger than the ranges that run close to but at right angles to them – notably Kakanui Mountains and Hawkdun and Old Man Ranges.

The Otago schist collision zone reaches the sea at Brighton, where creamy or orange sand mingles with outcrops of schist in or just above the tidal zone. The schist here is 130-140 million years old.

The Underlying Story 19

Explosive History

A lopsided depression or basin on Foulden Hill Station at the southern end of Taieri Ridge is the only hint of a crater lake that once existed here – the product of a volcanic eruption some 20 million years ago, seven million years before the great shield volcano began building on the coast.

The crater formed after magma from a vent interacted explosively with groundwater, which flashed to steam. As the explosions continued and more material was thrown out to form a lip or tuff ring, the hole grew steadily deeper. It is known as a Maar crater (after a region in Germany which has similar volcanic features). Rainwater filled it after cooling and the result was a lake about 1km wide and probably over 200m deep.

The lake became a forest-bound oasis for aquatic plant life. The stillness of the water was a feature, with drainage into it limited by the flatness of the surrounding peneplain. Tiny siliceous diatoms, green algae and freshwater sponges flourished and died – countless blooms and generations of them – and their remains sank gently to the lake bed, building up layers of sediment. As leaves from the fringing trees and shrubs fell into the water and sank to the bottom, they became encased in the sediment layers.

The leaves emerge today from the layers of diatomite (diatomaceous earth) as fossils, many of them breathtakingly intact and coloured in autumn hues. There are no trees of their species left. They are all extinct. Test drilling through the diatomite has reached 40m without finding the bottom of the deposit – an indication of the long life of the lake and the abundance of plant life in it. Probably the lake existed for over 100,000 years.

Volcanic rocks outcrop on two features nearby – Conical Hill (Smooth Cone) and two knobs at the end of Taieri Ridge called The Sisters. Further north on Taieri Ridge is

♦ The Caversham tunnel on the main trunk railway line penetrates Caversham Sandstone that lies 250m thick under the volcanic rocks of Lookout Point.

♦ In August 1979, at the suburb of Abbotsford, a large block of sand and clay up to 30m thick and covering about 18ha, moved 50m downslope in half an hour – a natural disaster that was headlined around the world. Sixty-nine houses were lost in the Abbotsford landslide, and 450 residents displaced.

♦ Shale near Waitati is oil-bearing. But no one has struck it rich.

Above: *Fossil Turret shells, and (left) leaf fossils, Foulden Hill.*

The Crater, which was formed explosively, like the one at Foulden Hill, and is much more recognisable as a crater. The sandstone remnants preserved in the vicinity of The Crater are a memento of an incursion by the sea, when the region was a peneplain. The sandstone has been dated at about 40 million years, but the volcanic rocks here are about 20 million years old.

♦ Coal seams, formed from plant remains in low-lying wetlands, occur in layers of sedimentary rock known as the Taratu Formation, which dates back 75 million years.

♦ Much of the commercially mined sand and gravel also lie in the Taratu sequence. The sand, mainly quartz, is valued for its decorative (white or cream) and hard-wearing nature. The quartz originated in the schist bedrock. Being schist's hardest component part, it was left after all the flaky parts were blown or washed away.

♦ Dark volcanic rocks with a greenish hue are phonolite. A good example is the massive outcrop supporting the Otago Peninsula Soldiers' Memorial off Highcliff Road, 225m above the harbour. Phonolite contains the mineral nepheline.

Chapter 3   OTAGO PENINSULA Nature's flagship

A map of the Otago Peninsula, showing places mentioned in the text, appears on page 47.

An island in the distant past, Otago Peninsula retains an identity peculiarly its own. Given Dunedin's status as a wildlife capital, the Peninsula is surely central square, a showpiece area with flags flying boldly and colourfully – the flags of rarity, special character and spectacular appeal. From a sharp outer end called Pukekura (Taiaroa Head) right back to the imposing bluffs of Highcliff and Vauxhall, the Peninsula is a gathering place for a strange mixture of animal life, some land-bound but much of it dependent on the sea. All roads lead to the Peninsula, it would seem. 'Magnetic' is a word that springs to mind, but 'strategic' is rather more accurate.

The Peninsula's indented shores lie close to deep water. Food is handy for the seabirds and marine mammals based on the beaches, rock platforms, cliffs and islets. Off the Peninsula, a series of submarine canyons narrows the continental shelf and brings deep water as close as 10km to the land. North and south of the Peninsula, the continental shelf widens to 30km. The canyons have long puzzled geologists. There is a theory they were created at a time of lower sea levels in the last five million years, when rivers extended out over the continental shelf.

Today the sea is getting its own back. It makes deep inroads into the Peninsula in the form of two large tidal inlets – Papanui and Hoopers. Their flatness is surprising amidst a landscape so hilly. The Peninsula's highest hills, in the order of 300-400m, are noticeably lower than the Mt Cargill group on the opposite side of the harbour, which were formed later in the era of volcanism and have been eroded to a lesser degree. On the Peninsula the hills are rounded and softened, a reminder that erosion, like rust,

Left: Prime elements of Otago Peninsula. Top to bottom: Harbour Cone, The Pyramids, Ongaonga or Tree nettle, Red admiral butterfly, Yellow-eyed penguin in Marram grass, Royal albatross, New Zealand fur seal, Variable oystercatcher.

Neville Peat

Right: Wild coast – Allans Beach and Cape Saunders from the Sandymount Wildlife Refuge. Mahoe forest is in the foreground. The prominent hill is Mt Charles (408m), Otago Peninsula's highest point.

is persistent and, given time, will dismantle and transform a landscape. Helping to soften the landscape is a clay robe of loess – wind-blown silt.

The highest peaks are Mt Charles (408m), Peggy's Hill (395m), the transmitter hill (381m), Sandymount (319m) and Harbour Cone (315m). Landslides on these and other Peninsula hills continue the process of erosion. The Peninsula is especially vulnerable to slips. Half of the area's 9,000 ha is at moderate to very severe risk of landslides. About 500 slip sites are recorded.

There are basically two sides to the landscape character of the Peninsula: the ocean coast, wild and wave-tossed, interspersing dark uncompromising cliffs of volcanic rock with lonely stretches of fine shifting sand; and the harbour shores, mainly rocky and with many sheltered places, where the sea has a gentler impact and washes a rock wall protecting a main road. A hilly backbone runs the length of the Peninsula – about 20km. Maximum width is 10km – a transect between Portobello Peninsula and Cape Saunders.

Human settlement has favoured the sun-catching harbour edge, much-modified now by ribbon development connecting the villages of Macandrew Bay, Broad Bay, Portobello, Harwood, Otakou and Harington Point. Harbour ferries served these places in the days before tarseal, when the Peninsula was a backwater crowded with dairy farms. The dairy farms have gone but they left their mark in the form of pastures, some enclosed by drystone basalt walls, and shelter belts of Monterey cyprus or Macrocarpa, the ubiquitous *Cupressus macrocarpa*. Highcliff Road, along the summit ridge of the Peninsula, has some magnificent stands of these trees.

The ferry-borne visitors of yesteryear regarded the likes of Broad Bay as a holiday resort. Today's visitors are quicker moving and they come for different reasons. They come to see natural wonders – albatrosses at the world's only mainland colony, a private sort of penguin called Yellow-eyed or Hoiho, and the fur seal and sea lions that are making a comeback on the mainland. People are attracted, too, by landscape features such as the collapsed sea chasm of Lovers' Leap near Sandymount (a leap of 220m!) and the wave-worn stacks of columnar basalt behind Victory Beach known as The Pyramids. They also come to see built heritage in the form of Larnach Castle, 302m above sea level, surrounded by lawn, flowerbeds and tall exotic trees, and the woodland gardens of Glenfalloch, which retain elements of the native forest that cloaked the Peninsula to the harbour edge. Glenfalloch's large matai tree, several hundred years old, is an arresting reminder of the forest that once grew here.

Although farmland still dominates the picture, the sur-

TOP TEN
Seabirds breeding in or around Taiaroa Head:

Royal albatross/Toroa
Diomedea epomophora

Blue penguin/Korora
Eudyptula minor

Yellow-eyed penguin/Hoiho
Megadyptes antipodes

Spotted shag/Parekareka
Stictocarbo punctatus

Stewart Island shag
Leucocarbo chalconotus

Little shag/Kawaupaka
Phalacrocorax melanoleucos

Sooty shearwater/Titi
Puffinus griseus

White-fronted tern/Tara
Sterna striata

Southern Black-backed gull/Karoro
Larus dominicanus

Red-billed gull /Tarapunga
Larus novaehollandiae

viving patches of native forest and shrubland are mostly under some form of protection. They are cherished not only for their component species, but also for their capacity to provide a home for penguins, Jewelled geckos, Red admiral butterflies and other fauna.

All in all, the Peninsula is a nature precinct with a high profile. It is a busy natural crossroads – a flagship of biodiversity.

Chris Gaskin

Above: *Pukekura Pa – an artist's reconstruction of Taiaroa Head 300 years ago, when a fortified village occupied it. Royal albatrosses are assumed to be breeding in the vicinity. The vessel returning home is a deep-sea fishing craft, a waka unua which specialised in catching barracouta.*

Seabird City

On the Otago Peninsula coast, seabirds abound. The air around Pukekura is filled with shags (cormorants), gulls and albatrosses throughout daylight hours in the breeding season. As darkness falls, Sooty shearwaters or Titi come home to their burrows, flying with swift, darting precision and an extraordinary energy for birds that have been out at sea fishing all day.

No two species fly alike. The shags are the commuters of this seabird city, going urgently about their business, often in line formation and flapping hard with necks outstretched. Gulls, floating on the wind, seem less driven by feeding or other schedules. Royal albatrosses, stiff-winged gliders of extraordinary size, perform graceful circuits of the headland, as if awaiting clearance from air-traffic control to land.

Three species of shag breed at this busy headland – Spotted, Stewart Island and Little. Little shags or Kawaupaka, the smallest of them, feed in the harbour and nest in foreshore trees. Their roosting on boatsheds, ramps, powerlines and trees on the harbour edge of the Peninsula is habitual. Stewart Island shags, found only in southern New Zealand, have entirely different habits, nesting in tight colonies on pedestals of mud and vegetation. Their Taiaroa Head colony

Above: *A Royal albatross skims the ocean off Taiaroa Head. The extent of black on the back of its wings suggests that it is under eight years of age.*

is the largest on the mainland. Up to 400 nests are occupied. Spotted shags or Parekareka nest on cliff ledges facing the ocean.

Sooty shearwaters (muttonbirds) go underground to breed, burrowing into sandy soils on suitable headlands. Because their mainland numbers have declined markedly through harvesting and land-use changes since the arrival of humans, the Peninsula population is of vital importance.

Otago Peninsula is also a stronghold for Yellow-eyed and Blue penguins. Yellow-eyeds, one of the world's rarest penguins, breed in shrubland on many of the Peninsula's ocean beaches and unlike most penguin species they stay based at their nesting areas after breeding is over for the year. Blue penguins nest in burrows or rock crevices. Some 200 nests are found around Taiaroa Head, which holds the largest concentration in Otago and one of the largest in New Zealand.

In addition, Southern Black-backed and Red-billed gulls, the commonest seabirds on the coast, breed on many headlands on the Peninsula. Fewer in number, White-fronted terns nest on cliff edges and also, surprisingly, on wooden posts at the Mole opposite Taiaroa Head. Of slender build, they fly with superb skill, often dipping their bills into the sea in flight to take prey.

All this seabird activity lends weight to New Zealand's claim as seabird capital of the world. No other country has a greater variety of seabirds breeding on its shores. Fully 70 percent of the 180 bird species breeding in the New Zealand region are seabirds, and Otago Peninsula is home to some of the most interesting.

Right: *Variable oystercatcher.*

THE ROYALS

The Royal albatross or Toroa is among the largest and most majestic of all seabirds, with a wingspan of about 3m and a flying style that enables it to traverse vast tracts of ocean quickly and efficiently.

There are two subspecies – Northern and Southern. Breeding is confined to the New Zealand region, although they range widely through the great Southern Ocean and probably circumnavigate it on a regular basis. More than 80 percent of their lives is spent at sea, which is their tuckshop, watering hole and waterbed. The small Taiaroa Head colony was established by Northern Royal albatrosses, whose main breeding sites are found in the Chatham Islands over 1,000km north-east of Dunedin. Some 7,000 pairs nest there. In 1938, when the first chick in modern times flew from Taiaroa Head, there were three breeding pairs; now there are about 25. The total population (adults, sub-adults and juveniles) is about 100.

Royal albatrosses are long-lived and slow to reproduce. They may not start breeding until they are eight to 10 years old and, if successful, will raise only one chick every second year. They 'holiday' at sea between breeding years. The breeding season starts in October, with their arrival back at the colony and a reuniting of the pair. Eggs are laid in November and incubated for about 80 days – a world record for seabirds. The chick is guarded and fed by each parent in turn for the first five weeks, after which both parents are fully employed catching food for it. At fledging, usually in September, the chick may be heavier than its parents, at over 8kg. When it eventually takes to the air, it will spend at least three years at sea before returning to the colony.

Squid are prominent in the diet of Royal albatrosses, which feed by seizing prey at the surface, often at night. Up to about a quarter of the diet of Taiaroa Head-based birds is octopus, much of which is probably scavenged from fishing boats. The Royal's large bill is adapted for hooking and slicing squid. The tubes at the top are nostrils, through which excess salt is drained from the bird's salt glands.

The Taiaroa Head albatrosses have been continuously studied for decades – longer than any other seabird. A female banded as an adult breeding bird in the 1930s lived for over 60 years, setting a world age record for a wild bird. 'Grandma' disappeared in 1989, with a chick at the nest. The chick fledged, thanks to some hand feeding, and has since returned to the colony as a juvenile.

Few of the world's seabirds are as intensively managed as Dunedin's Royals. Although free to come and go, they are closely monitored. Eggs are weighed for sign of infertility; hatching is assisted occasionally; chicks are weighed and orphans assigned foster parents; supplementary feeding is

'Beachmaster'

The bird world's equivalent of a beachmaster is the Variable oystercatcher or Torea-pango *Haematopus unicolor*. Commonly called Black Oystercatcher, it sets up territories along Otago Peninsula beaches in the breeding season (November to January), and expresses annoyance at any intrusion – a sharp piping call. Two or three eggs are laid in a simple nest, often nothing more than a scrape in the sand at or just above high water.

Most sandy beaches on the Peninsula are packed with Black oystercatcher territories, shoulder to shoulder. The Variable oystercatcher comes in a pied form, but black ones prevail in southern New Zealand. The pied Variable may be confused with South Island Pied oystercatcher but the latter is in fact a different species, almost always nesting inland.

In winter, Black oystercatchers gather in flocks to feed. A regular low-tide haunt is the rocky cove at Vauxhall. At high tide they invade sports fields, including the one at Tomahawk, in search of worms, grubs and other invertebrates.

George Chance

instituted when required. In addition, routine trapping for predators (cats, ferrets, stoats, rats) is carried out and precautions are taken against flystrike at hatching time.

As a result of this hands-on management by Department of Conservation staff at the 5ha Taiaroa Head Nature Reserve, the Royal albatross population is probably 25 birds better off.

The colony was established in the 1930s following the protective work of a Dunedin teacher and ornithologist, Lance Richdale. Since 1972, it has been open to public viewing.

Albatross Family

Except for three species in the North Pacific and one based in the Galapagos Islands at the Equator, albatrosses are southern seabirds. Ten species, including the mollymawks, breed in the south. No fewer than seven of them breed in New Zealand's temperate and subantarctic zones, among them the largest albatrosses of all – the Wandering and Royal.

Buller's mollymawk *Diomedea bulleri* and White-capped (Shy) mollymawk *Diomedea cauta* are occasionally sighted, patrolling inshore waters off Otago Peninsula.

The term mollymawk is interchangeable with albatross.

Below: *Department of Conservation staff Isobel Burns (left) and Sandra McGrouther weigh a Royal albatross egg to check for infertility. The egg will lose moisture at a prescribed rate throughout incubation. A dummy egg is placed under the bird while the real one is weighed. The Richdale Observatory, from which members of the public view the colony, is at left.*

Neville Peat

Keeping Track

In the 1993-4 breeding season, two nesting birds at the Taiaroa Head colony took part in a novel experiment aimed at tracking albatross flightpaths and understanding more about their foraging habits.

Tiny electronic packages, tuned to satellites, were attached to their backs and later recovered. Besides transmitting each bird's location, the packages measured air speed, barometric pressure, temperature and movements such as flying, feeding and sitting.

One of the birds, a male, performed three flights with the gear. It covered 739km on the longest flight, which took six days. The tracks taken by these two birds suggested the Taiaroa Head albatrosses, early in the season, tend to feed near the edge of the continental shelf adjacent to the Otago coast in water 500m to 1000m deep.

They do not seem to fly as far for food as, say, the Wandering albatrosses of the Auckland Islands, three of which had transmitter packages attached later in the season. They flew deep into the Tasman Sea, covering thousands of kilometres in a flight. Information from this and similar experiments elsewhere in the Southern Ocean is assisting scientists studying the alarming number of albatrosses killed by deep-water longline fishing operations (when the birds scavenge for bait and are hooked).

Conservationists have been campaigning for some years to change fishing gear and practices in an effort to reduce the albatross bycatch. Forest and Bird have taken a leading role in this campaign.

SUBURBIA FOR SHAGS

Surrounding the Royal albatross colony on every side are the nesting areas of three shag (cormorant) species, each requiring a different habitat.

On the cliffs on the ocean side, sleek Spotted shags plait nests of seaweed, usually on narrow ledges and about 1m apart. On average, three eggs are laid, but breeding success varies. Every few years adults die in significant numbers, probably because of a sudden decline in their food resources. They prey on schools of small fish over the continental shelf, diving foot-propelled to about 20m, usually in groups.

Stewart Island shags, largest of the three species (wingspan 1.2m and up to 3kg in weight), nest on columns of mud-compacted seaweed and grass up to half a metre tall. The only mainland colony of this endemic southern New Zealand species is located at Taiaroa Head, overlooking Aramoana. It contains about 400 nests, tightly packed. One or two chicks are fledged per nest. There are pied and bronze (entirely dark) forms.

Setnet Threat

Monofilament gillnets, set to catch fish in Otago Harbour or off the coast, can entangle and drown marine fauna such as shags, penguins, dolphins and seals.

Spotted shags entering Otago Harbour seasonally in large groups in pursuit of shoaling fish are especially at risk. Yellow-eyed and Blue penguins have also been killed in nets in the past, while commuting between their beaches and offshore feeding grounds.

As a result of the toll on non-target species, setnets are banned from designated sections of the Peninsula coastline and parts of Otago Harbour. Conservation groups are campaigning for an extension of the banned areas to cover most of the Peninsula coast and all of the harbour.

Right: *Stewart Island shag colony, Taiaroa Head.*

High-rise, high-density living: Spotted shags nesting at Taiaroa Head. The grey back feathers have dark tips, which give a spotted appearance. At courtship these birds have striking crested plumage around the head.

Like Spotted shags, Stewart Island shags feed mainly at sea. They can stay submerged for up to 3min while diving to at least 50m, in pursuit of bottom-dwelling fish as well as mid-water ones.

Little shags, weighing under 1kg, nest in trees on the harbour side of the headland, being essentially harbour-dwelling. They lay 3-4 eggs. For unknown reasons, only about half the adult population on the harbour will breed in any one year.

A typical sight on Otago Harbour as they roost on trees or structures overhanging the water, Little shags dive for fish to depths of about 5m. Their dives last up to half a minute. They are often seen with wings hung out to dry. Their plumage is black and white – black backs, white fronts – although the degree of white on undersurfaces varies.

BLUE PENGUIN Small is Beautiful

Blue penguins or Korora nest at several places on Otago Peninsula, but nowhere as abundantly as at Taiaroa Head. In the mid-1980s there were only 30 to 50 nests; within 10 years the number had jumped to 200. Most are located within the nature reserve or just outside it at Pilot's Beach.

The smallest penguins of all, Blues *Eudyptula minor*, weigh just over 1kg and have a body length of about 30cm. They are found throughout New Zealand, although predation by cats, dogs and mustelids has reduced their numbers significantly on the mainland. Predator trapping at Taiaroa Head to protect the Royal albatrosses has probably benefited the population of Blues. Wooden nesting boxes have been installed to encourage them and provide further protection.

Blues nest in burrows or caves, often in association with other burrowing seabirds, and they set out to raise two chicks – sometimes a second brood in the same year. At sea, usually in groups, they pursue mid-water fish and squid. Still in groups, they return to shore after dusk. Their loud screeching and braying calls at night have made them unpopular with crib owners in the past.

HOIHO A Private Sort of Penguin

Otago Peninsula is a stronghold for the Yellow-eyed penguin or Hoiho. Over half the South Island population lives here.

At 70cm tall and over 5kg in weight, hoiho is the largest penguin living in a temperate region – South Island east coast and Stewart Island. Yellow-eyeds also breed at subantarctic Auckland Islands and Campbell Island. Periodic declines in population due to food shortages, biotoxins in the food web or predation by mustelids, dogs and cats at mainland breeding areas, have prompted the species to be dubbed the world's rarest penguin.

Unlike most of the world's 18 penguin species, Hoiho prefer to nest out of view of neighbours. They nest on the ground in coastal dune vegetation, shrubland or forest and will walk hundreds of metres, over sometimes steep terrain, to reach a suitable nest site.

A non-migratory species, they tend to go to sea during daylight hours to feed and return to the breeding area, their natal site, in the late afternoon. During the breeding season their routines may vary. Yellow-eyeds usually mate with the previous season's partner. Two eggs are laid by September, with the six-week incubation shared. Chicks are guarded in turn by the parents for about six weeks, then left by themselves during the day while the parents go out fishing. Fledging occurs some 15 weeks after hatching. Juveniles typically test out their brand-new feather wetsuits with a journey north, as far as the Cook Strait region, in their first year.

After February, when the chicks fledge, the adult birds fatten themselves in preparation for their annual moult. They must stay out of the water for about two weeks, until their old feathers have been replaced entirely by a new set. During moulting the birds may appear unwell. They are vulnerable to dog attacks and fire at this time. If chased into the sea without their insulating feathers intact, they will die of exposure.

Out on its Own

Hoiho, the Yellow-eyed, is the best-known of the six penguin species breeding in New Zealand – three on the mainland (Yellow-eyed, Fiordland crested and Blue), three in the subantarctic zone (Snares crested, Erect crested and Rockhopper).

It is also the most distinct penguin scientifically, justifying a genus of its own – *Megadyptes antipodes*, meaning large southern diver. It is regarded as the least adapted in size, bone structure and feathering of all the penguins; in other words, it is the penguin most closely related to ancestral members of the family.

Penguins go back a long way. Fossil discoveries in New

Right: *A moulting Yellow-eyed penguin with a fledgling. Moulted feathers float in a rock pool. Moulting occurs after breeding.*

Hoiho Trust
Annual seminars run by the Trust have attracted an array of groups and organisations with a commitment to conserving the Yellow-eyed penguin on the mainland, including the Royal Forest and Bird Protection Society, Worldwide Fund for Nature, University of Otago, Mainland Products Ltd, Otago Museum and the Department of Conservation. In New Zealand, no other native bird species has attracted as much publicity about its plight as the Yellow-eyed penguin.

Zealand point to a 'proto-penguin' that lived 50 to 60 million years ago. It almost certainly evolved from seabirds that flew. Since then, penguins have adapted in astonishing ways to become the bird world's most accomplished swimmers and divers.

High-Profile Bird

Since its rarity and unusual nature came to public notice in the 1980s, the Yellow-eyed penguin has become a nation-wide symbol of conservation. The Yellow-eyed Penguin Trust was launched in Dunedin in 1987 in response to concern about the future of the species on the mainland. That concern was highlighted by population studies of mainland colonies undertaken by Otago Museum zoologist John Darby, starting in 1980 and following on from the pioneering work of Lance Richdale. In the years since its formation, the Trust has been a rallying point for wide-ranging conservation efforts.

Conservation strategies include habitat purchase, revegetation programmes, nesting boxes, predator trapping, ongoing scientific studies, fundraising and education.

MARINE MAMMALS Cruising

Marine mammals – fur seals, sea lions, dolphins and whales – are attracted to the waters around Otago Peninsula for the same reason that seabirds congregate here: food supply.

New Zealand fur seals are now plentiful in the area. In small numbers, Hooker's sea lions are beginning to make their presence felt on the beaches. Dolphins and whales are less obvious – unless they strand.

Three species of dolphin enter Otago Harbour occasionally – Dusky, Bottlenose and Common. Dusky dolphins, the most commonly encountered species in New Zealand coastal waters, are relatively abundant off Otago in winter and spring. The dolphins that swim up the harbour as far as Dunedin are most likely to be Bottlenose dolphin, or the smaller Common dolphin. Common dolphins may perform spectacular leaps.

Orcas (Killer whales) are rarer off the Peninsula. In 1992 a pod of 12 Orcas cruised around the Otago Harbour entrance. Southern right whales have been seen inside the entrance in the past. Before commercial whaling slashed their numbers, they possibly used the sheltered waters of the harbour for calving.

Occasional visitors to Peninsula shores are Leopard seal and Elephant seal.

Graeme Loh

Left: *A Southern Right whale wallowing off Otago Peninsula in winter, 1994. A group of four Right whales spent several weeks in the vicinity of the Peninsula, prompting speculation they might be breeding. Right whales swim slowly – four knots is a sprint. They feed on krill.*

NEW ZEALAND FUR SEAL A flourishing act

Otago Peninsula is a showpiece area for the New Zealand fur seal *Arctocephalus forsteri*.

Before 1970 the fur seal population was small and scattered. Breeding began about 1980 and has been steadily increasing since. There are now breeding colonies all along the Peninsula, notably at Cape Saunders and Taiaroa Head, and numerous haul-out sites. In the 1993-4 breeding season the Peninsula colonies produced about 1200 pups, according to a census carried out by scientists.

For breeding habitat, fur seals favour sea caves and rocky shelves out of reach of waves. Haul-out sites, including gravel beaches and rock islets, may be more exposed. Adjacent grassy or tussock-clad slopes are often used for resting, sleeping or convalescing from injuries.

From late October breeding males, weighing up to 185kg, set up territories and fight hard to hold them. Females give birth in December, mating with the territory-holder about a week later. The pup is dependent on its mother for almost a year. Tagging studies suggest there is some movement between Otago Peninsula and the West Coast. Males disperse northward after breeding but females, which are difficult to tell apart from sub-adult males, stay within range of the breeding sites. Numbers peak in late summer.

Fur seal populations are in the process of recovering from mainland extinction by Maori hunters in pre-European times and by early European sealers. Eventually, their numbers will be limited by the availability of suitable breeding habitat.

Arrow squid and octopus make up more than half the diet of fur seals, which feed mainly at night. Diving to over 200m, they also eat fish, mainly hoki, barracouta and lanternfish.

Performing in the Wild

One of the best places to view fur seals from land is at Taiaroa Head.

On the headland's ocean side, the seals haul out on to broad rock platforms and are commonly seen frolicking in tidal rock pools or swimming along the shore. Close-up viewing is available at Pilots Beach on the harbour side of the headland, a favourite haul-out site for males young and old.

Harbour cruise vessels offer good views of the seals from the water.

Neville Peat

Right: *Fur seals hauled out at Pipikaretu Point, where Bull kelp swirls in the surging sea. Fur seals, dark grey to grey-brown, are covered in fine dense fur. They have a pointed snout, long whiskers and small external ears. Colonial breeders, they also congregate outside the breeding season.*

HOOKER'S SEA LION Comeback story

The rarest of the world's five sea lion species, Hooker's sea lion *Phocarctos hookeri* is making a comeback on mainland New Zealand – and Otago Peninsula is centre stage.

Eliminated by Maori hunters from the mainland before the arrival of Europeans, these sea lions are seen singly or in small groups on the Peninsula's sandy beaches and dunelands. The southern end of Victory Beach is a regular haul-out site, but they may appear on any beach. Population studies in 1994 suggested that up to about 20 may be ashore at any one time. Similar numbers are using the Catlins beaches, the only other mainland area attracting them at present. The majority are young males – migrants from the species' main breeding sites in the subantarctic Auckland Islands. Mainland breeding colonies have yet to form, but regular breeding may occur by the late 1990s.

Elephant Seals

Southern Elephant seals *Mirounga leonina* visit Otago Peninsula occasionally. Taiaroa Head and Te Rauone Beach at Harington Point are among the haul-out sites for these seals, which sometimes become traffic hazards on Harington Point Road.

Elephant seals haul out on sand or gravel beaches to breed, moult or rest. While moulting (skin and hair peels off in patches), they may stay out of the water for a couple of weeks. The nearest breeding site is Nugget Point, South Otago, but most breeding occurs on subantarctic islands.

They are the world's largest seal, with adult males reaching over 5m in length and four tonnes in weight. They have an enlarged nose or proboscis, from which they get their name. Females are much smaller. On land, elephant seals are slow and cumbersome, resembling giant caterpillars, but at sea they can dive to depths of over one kilometre in pursuit of fish and other prey.

Left: *Hooker's sea lions on Papanui Beach.*

Bulls can weigh over 400kg – twice the weight of fur seal males – and reach about 3m in length, with long hair over neck and shoulders forming a lion-like mane. They are distinguished from fur seals by their greater size, blunt head and short whiskers. Their gait differs, too. Fur seals gallop; sea lions march steadily on all fours, moving their legs in turn. Female sea lions, much smaller and paler than adult males and sometimes creamy, are difficult to tell apart from males under two years of age.

Sea lions prefer sand to rock. A layer of blubber (rather than fur) insulates them, and to keep cool when ashore they often hunker down in the sand and flick it over their backs with their flippers, till they are almost buried.

Diet studies identify barracouta, red cod, flounder and jack mackerel as important fish. Skate, octopus and paddle crab also feature in sea lion diet. Like fur seals, sea lions are highly agile in the water and dive to over 200m.

The total population of Hooker's sea lions is in the range of 10,000 to 15,000. Alarm over the numbers being caught in the nets of squid trawlers operating in subantarctic seas has led to changes in fishing gear and practices.

Denis Pagé

Right: *Born famous: This female Hooker's sea lion pup created wildlife history when she was born near Taieri Mouth in December 1993 – the first known successful breeding on the mainland in post-European times. She sheltered in dune shrubland for about three months before going to sea, escorted by her mother. Over the next few weeks the pair made their way north. They chose Victory Beach as their main base for the rest of the year.*

PENINSULA PLANT LIFE Exclusive elements

In keeping with the distinctive nature of the fauna and the island atmosphere of the place, plant life on Otago Peninsula boasts some exceptional and exclusive elements.

As one might expect of a large island, the vegetation map is a mosaic of plant communities, ranging from cliff vegetation and coastal turf through shrublands on dunes, damp places and drier slopes to forests of flowering trees and, oldest community of all, tall podocarps. The suite of trees and shrubs (including the shrubs *Corokia cotoneaster*, *Helichrysum aggregatum* and *Carmichaelia virgata*) is commensurate with a drier and sunnier climate than that found on the higher, wetter hills on the other side of the harbour.

The good news is that diversity still rules; on the sadder side is the fact that little more than a tenth (about 1,000ha) of the Peninsula is still forested, only half of it native.

Tall forest once clothed the Peninsula to the cliff edges and dunelands, dominated by the magnificent podocarps – Rimu, Miro, Matai, Totara and Kahikatea. Most of it was felled for building timber and fence posts following European settlement, and pasture was sown in its place.

Once the predominant community, podocarp forest is now the rarest. On the lower slopes of Harbour Cone (Hereweka) overlooking Hoopers Inlet is the last surviving stand of Rimu *Dacrydium cupressinum* – a grove of about 60 trees up to 15m tall and half a metre in trunk diameter. Interspersed with some ten large specimens of Pokaka *Elaeocarpus hookerianus*, the Rimu survive amid a 10ha patch of Kanuka-dominant bush, the whole a fetching snapshot of Otago Peninsula of old, with animal life to reinforce the picture. The Rimu enclave is home to families of Rifleman, a native bush bird, New Zealand's smallest. Less obvious is a species of lacewing peculiar to podocarp forest.

Below: *The shrub* Helichrysum aggregatum *is an important host to several insect species. This elegant moth –* Celama parvitis *– would be almost invisible on the underside of the leaves of its larval food plant.*

The Peninsula's largest patch of native forest is Taiaroa Bush, covering 42ha of hillside bordering Okia Flat. The large podocarps have gone (there remain only a few small examples of Hall's Totara *Podocarpus hallii* and Matai or Black pine *Prumnopitys taxifolia*), but the Peninsula's commonest native trees are here – the ubiquitous Mahoe or Whiteywood *Melicytus ramiflorus*, coast-loving Ngaio *Myoporum laetum*, gully-hugging Tree Fuchsia or Kotukutuku *Fuchsia exorticata*, and Broadleaf *Griselinia littoralis*, which tolerates most conditions, including dry sites on its own. Narrow-leaved Lacebark *Hoheria angustifolia* are among the tallest trees of Taiaroa Bush. Kowhai *Sophora microphylla* gilds the forest in spring with its flowers.

Other flowering trees here, all of which produce berries, are Milk tree or Turepo *Streblus heterophyllus*, Putaputaweta or Marbleleaf *Carpodetus serratus*, and Wineberry or Makomako *Aristotelia serrata*. Among the shrubs, the coprosmas are well represented by *Coprosma areolata*, *C. rubra* and *C. crassifolia*. The vines of Supplejack *Ripogonum scandens* and *Muehlenbeckia australis* add a tangled, unruly appearance.

Overall, though, the understorey has been too exposed to stock from adjacent farmland over many years to develop its natural complexity – a familiar experience for patches of native bush in many other parts of the Peninsula.

Across the Peninsula, gullies too steep to plough, or too shady and damp to be of much use to farming, are refuges for shrubs and small trees. Among the common species are the coprosmas *Coprosma propinqua* and *C. rotundifolia*, Kohuhu *Pittosporum tenuifolium*, Mingimingi *Cyathodes*

Above: *The Lacewing* Micromus bifasciatus *is an attractive if rarely seen inhabitant of the Hereweka Rimu.*

Above: *This stand of Rimu and Pokaka, on the lower slopes of Harbour Cone (Hereweka) overlooking Hoopers Inlet, is unique on Otago Peninsula. It is protected within a private covenant. This forest remnant provides habitat for the diminutive Rifleman which survives at a few places on the Peninsula, including this patch, where nesting boxes are put out.*

Tall forest once clothed the Otago Peninsula to the cliff edges and dunelands, dominated by the magnificent podocarps – Rimu, Miro, Matai, Totara and Kahikatea.

juniperina, Pepper tree or Horopito *Pseudowintera colorata*, Mapou *Myrsine australis* and Koromiko or New Zealand Veronica *Hebe salicifolia*.

At Sandymount, south of Hoopers Inlet, there is a real mixture of plant communities – low forest dominated in turn by Ngaio and Mahoe, a 10ha stand of Kanuka, and clifftop and coastal shrublands featuring *Coprosma crassifolia*, *Hebe elliptica*, Fierce lancewood *Pseudopanax ferox*, *Corokia cotoneaster* and the Tree nettle or Ongaonga *Urtica ferox*. Tree daisies are plentiful here – *Olearia arborescens* and *Olearia avicenniifolia* (Akeake). Both present bold showings of honey-scented white flowers, clouds of them – *O. arborescens* in early summer, its cousin at the end of summer.

On the southern side of Portobello Peninsula is a tree daisy anomaly. Clinging to cliffs near the Portobello Marine Laboratory are specimens of *Brachyglottis rotundifolia* or Muttonbird scrub, which is possibly out of place here and may have been introduced some decades ago. A relative of Muttonbird scrub, but with vastly different form, is the yellow-flowering liane *Brachyglottis sciadophila*. It is one of Otago Peninsula's special plants – a rare species close to its southern limit. Native scrambling species do well on the

Peninsula, with gaps having opened up for them as a result of the decimation of forest and the regrouping of remnant patches. The list includes Climbing Rata *Metrosideros diffusa*, native Jasmine *Parsonsia heterophylla*, leafless Lawyer *Rubus squarrosus*, and a relative of Kotukutuku, *Fuchsia perscandens*.

Five parasitic mistletoes are found in the Dunedin area, two of which are significant on the Peninsula – *Ileostylus micranthus* and the much smaller, easily over-looked *Korthalsella lindsayi*. The former grows on a range of native and introduced species, but coprosmas are a favourite host. Among the ground plants, orchids feature. There are 11 species on the Peninsula and they occupy a range of habitats, including forest, rock outcrops and banks. Sandymount is a haven for orchids, including the small yellow-flowered epiphyte *Drymoanthus flavum*, named in 1994.

Certain exotic trees and shrubs have a high profile on the Peninsula, notably the Monterey cypress *Cupressus macrocarpa*, shelter belts of which are everywhere to be seen festooned with the native fleshy fern *Pyrrosia eleagnifolia*, and Elderberry trees and Lupin, both of which spread freely, especially on sandy country. A disease hit Lupin in the late 1980s, causing widespread dieback and leaving many dunelands looking devastated. The disease, affecting the roots, is thought to be cyclical and causes periodic diebacks in the Lupin populations in the years ahead.

Often associated with stands of Lupin is a common shrub, Poroporo *Solanum laciniatum*, which reaches a height of 3-4m. In summer it bears elegant purple flowers followed by impressive yellow-orange fruit that resemble miniature tamarillos. The fruits often have a hole in them – the exit hole of the moth *Sceliodes cordalis*, whose caterpillar feeds within. Beware the unripe fruits. They are poisonous.

Marram grass *Ammophila arenaria*, an introduced species, now dominates the foredune vegetation – once the preserve of the native orange-leaved sand sedge Pingao *Desmoschoenus spiralis*. Pingao survives in only a few places, mainly on cliffs where marram grass cannot crowd it out, but several beaches are being replanted with Pingao through projects supported by Conservation Corps and Maori communities.

Protected areas

About 1,000ha (10 percent) of Otago Peninsula land is protected, with most reserves under Department of Conservation management.

The oldest reserve is the Sandfly Bay Wildlife Refuge (338ha), created in 1908. There are now protected areas on either side of it (Sandymount Recreation Reserve and Boulder Beach Conservation Area), and together they provide protection for the natural values on an 8km coastal

The Climbing daisy Brachyglottis sciadophila *flowering in March at Styles Creek Bush, Broad Bay.*

strip stretching from Highcliff to Allans Beach.

The Yellow-Eyed Penguin Trust in association with the Dunedin City Council manages a 231ha reserve at Okia Flat. The Trust also has a small reserve at Otekiho near Taiaroa Head.

Several private landholders have negotiated the placement of covenants over patches of bush on their properties. One example is the Peggys Hill patch, now fenced off from adjacent farmland. The bush here contains a few plants that have disappeared from most other parts of the Peninsula, including *Pseudopanax simplex* (Haumakoroa), *Coprosma foetidissima* (Hupiro), and Mountain Holly or Hakeke *Olearia ilicifolia*. Styles Bush at Broad Bay is another notable covenanted area, which is being enhanced by a replanting programme.

The City Council has a few small reserves and it also maintains a network of walking tracks on the Peninsula.

Cliff-dwellers

A significant number of Otago Peninsula's rare and special plant species occur on cliffs and coastal banks, no doubt because such habitats are protected by their inaccessibility.

Right: *The Cape Saunders rock daisy* Helichrysum intermedium *var.* tumidum, *an Otago Peninsula endemic.*

Neville Peat

Brian Patrick

The star turn is a rock daisy that is found nowhere else – *Helichrysum intermedium* var. *tumidum*, the Cape Saunders rock daisy. It clings to cliffs at Cape Saunders and a little further south at Sandymount. Its cylindrical stems, with tiny leaves tightly bound, appear swollen (tumid). A profusion of small pale-yellow flowers (December-January) at the tip of the stems highlights the rounded, compact form of the shrub, which seems secure in its habitat of lichen-encrusted cliffs. It is stouter than *H. intermedium*, which is found inland on rocky sites in the mountains.

Two native Forget-me-nots and a native Daphne are notable. The white-flowered southern Forget-me-not *Myosotis rakiura*, was rediscovered at Highcliff in recent years – its northernmost location. It was named after the Maori name for Stewart Island, where it is common. Its diminutive relative, *Myosotis pygmaea* var. *pygmaea* is found at only a few locations along Peninsula cliff tops. Both forget-me-nots flower over summer. The Daphne relative is the glaucous-leaved *Pimelea* aff. *urvilleana*, which is also restricted to a few cliff tops.

Some plants that are common high up in the mountains are established on Peninsula cliffs as well, among them the Grass tree or Inaka *Dracophyllum longifolium* and mat daisies that develop cushion-like form – *Raoulia australis*

Above: *Cliff-top vegetation at Cape Saunders featuring Silver tussock Poa cita, greenish-orange cushions of* Scleranthus uniflorus *and windshorn shrubs of* Melicytus crassifolius. *Also growing here are a variety of* Raoulia *species, compact small cushions of* Colobanthus muelleri *and other native herbs and grasses.*

and *Raoulia beauverdii*.

Common native cliff-dwellers include the ubiquitous Iceplant *Disphyma australe*, the yellow-flowering Shore groundsel *Senecio carnosulus* (type locality, Black Head), Coastal speedwell *Hebe elliptica*, and Shore Spinach *Tetragonia trigyna*, which drapes its fleshy leaves over rocks and other plants.

Providing a fluffy cap along the cliffs in many places is the handsome coastal Blue tussock *Poa astonii*.

Okia Flat

On Okia Flat behind the dunes of Victory Beach, the longest (4km) stretch of sand on the Peninsula, coastal turf and duneland plants abound.

Some of these are vulnerable, however. They include Sand Bidibid *Acaena pallida*, a low stout herb with reddish flowerheads. It is found at only two other sites in New Zealand beyond Otago Peninsula. A close relative, *Acaena novae-zelandiae*, is common.

The diminutive shrub Patotara *Leucopogon fraseri* forms straggly mats amid the grasses. Its fruits, orange and succulent when ripe, are deliciously sweet. On the foredunes are thickets of New Zealand Flax or Harakeke *Phormium tenax* (Phormium is from a Greek word for basket and refers to the Maori use of the leaves).

In the back-dune hollows of Okia Flat, an ephemeral wetland flora of rushes and sedges and the short turf areas support a distinctive assemblage of beetles, bugs and moths. Much of the fauna is diurnal, delighting to fly or run on the warmest days. It includes the following moths – the elegant crambid moth *Diasemia grammalis*, the pyralid *Delogenes limodoxa* and the geometrid *Arctesthes catapyrrha* are examples. The larvae of the last mentioned feed on *Nertera setulosa* here.

Below: *This flightless caddis – Pseudoeconesus paludis – is endemic to Dunedin and common on Otago Peninsula in seepages (such as at Okia Flat) surrounded by* Carex appressa *and other sedges. The only other known locality for it is a seepage at 700m on Swampy Summit. With both sexes flightless, these caddis are strong runners in a habitat where predacious water spiders* Dolomedes minor *abound.*

Brian Patrick

Cook's Scurvy Grass

A native cress *Lepidium oleraceum,* found at only a few sites on Otago Peninsula, is one of New Zealand's rarest herbs. It was used by Captain Cook as a vitamin C supplement in his crew's diet and thus was a remedy for scurvy. Consequently, it is known as Cook's Scurvy Grass. Highly palatable to stock and rabbits, it has become endangered. One of the last remaining populations is found in an unusual place – the Mole at Aramoana – which lends weight to a theory that it may need seabird droppings (guano) to survive.

Right: Lepidium oleraceum *in flower, Green Island. Related to the common cabbage, it is a host plant for the introduced Diamond-back moth and White butterfly.*

Neville Peat

This Muehlenbeckia moth Morova subfasciatus *has just emerged from the small hole on the stem (lower right). The larvae spend their entire lives inside the stems, causing a swelling to form in which they feed and eventually pupate. An escape route for the emerging adult is made by the caterpillar beforehand and the hole is covered with silk to hide it from the attentions of parasitic flies or wasps.*

Muehlenbeckia: An image problem

Ordinarily confined to the forest edge, *Muehlenbeckia australis* is a scrambling plant that is much maligned for its habit of cloaking remnant shrubland and regenerating forest. It is often regarded as a smothering weed, but merits a better image for the role it plays as a host to invertebrate fauna, including on Otago Peninsula two Copper butterflies and over 20 moth species. Stick insects and beetles are also fond of it.

Two sides to tree nettle

The Tree nettle *Urtica ferox* or Ongaonga is a plant to admire but not touch. Its white bristles contain three kinds of poison that will inflict a painful rash if brushed against. People repeatedly stung can become seriously ill. Ongaonga, which grows to about 3m in height, is common on bush margins and disturbed, semi-shaded sites. Watch out for it, especially on track margins at Sandymount and Highcliff.

There is another side to Ongaonga, though. It is used by Yellow-eyed penguins as breeding habitat and it is also popular with insects. It is a host plant for the majestic Red admiral butterfly, whose fat caterpillars not only feed on the leaves but also mimic the nettle by carrying around their own array of spines. When not feeding, the larvae shelter within a curled leaf and may later pupate there. Other insects attracted to nettle include a leaf-mining fly, two elegant geometrid moths, two noctuid moths and a brown pyraustine moth. The larvae of all of them feed on the foliage – rather carefully!

The much smaller nettle *Urtica incisa*, also native, is another important host for insects, but it is becoming rare now and is confined to a few bush remnants.

Marine Caddis: Odd one out

Most insects are land-based. Generally, they have left marine habitats to their arthropod relatives, the crustacea. Among the exceptions is the marine caddis, a group of five species related to moths and represented in Otago Harbour by one species.

The Peninsula caddis is *Philanisus plebeius*, a species shared with south-east Australia. The rocky shores between Portobello and Vauxhall support the southernmost population of this species. The other four known species of caddis dependent on the sea are endemic to discrete parts of New Zealand.

Adults tend to be active at night, flying around lights during summer evenings. By day they might rest on the undersides of boatsheds. The larvae are quite different. They construct a protective case from silk, decorated with rock-pool plants. This makes them very hard to find in the rock pools around the harbour where they feed on various algae species.

Caddis species associated with fresh water are prolific on Otago Peninsula, where some 15 species are recorded, some flightless, others diurnal.

Below: *A larval case of* Philanisus plebeius *in an Otago Harbour rock pool. Its black head protrudes from the case, which is about 15mm long.*

Scorpionflies and Stoneflies

The insect order Mecoptera (Scorpionflies) has only one New Zealand representative, *Nannochorista philpotti* (pictured below). It is common on Otago Peninsula, where its elongate larvae feed in the mud of slow-moving streams.

In common with stoneflies, mayflies and caddis, the scorpionfly depends on fresh water for larval growth. But the adults of all these groups shun the aquatic life, preferring to live in streamside vegetation or on rocks.

Stoneflies, although fully winged, characteristically prefer to walk rather than fly. No fewer than 10 species of stonefly have been recorded from the Peninsula. The commonest include a long-winged brown lowland variety of *Zelandobius foxi* and its fast-moving congener, *Z. uniramus*.

Jewelled Gecko

The brilliantly coloured Jewelled gecko *Naultinus gemmeus*, a species of green tree gecko found only in the South Island, is one of Otago Peninsula's rarer inhabitants.

Reaching 18cm in length, this gecko lives in shrubland, chiefly bushes of twiggy, small-leaved *Coprosma propinqua*. Using its tail to hold on, it will drape itself over outer branches on sunny days, waiting to catch passing insects. Young are born live in early winter, usually two at a time.

Like New Zealand's seven other species of diurnal tree gecko, the Jewelled gecko is well camouflaged. It is predominantly green, with yellow or white stripes running lengthwise, often interspersed with diamond-shaped splotches.

The species is found east of the main divide between Banks Peninsula and Nugget Point, with Otago Peninsula a stronghold for it. Small populations occur at more than 20 places on the Peninsula.

Concern over the Jewelled gecko's status and diminished habitat led to the creation of a small (0.85ha) reserve on fragmented shrubland near Broad Bay in 1993. Named the Every Scientific Reserve after the former owners of the property, Paul and Phyllis Every, it was jointly funded by the Marjorie Barclay Trust (through Royal Forest and Bird Protection Society), Save The Otago Peninsula Inc, and Department of Conservation. Now fenced to keep out cats and mustelids, the reserve protects one of the last significant populations of Jewelled gecko on the Peninsula – an estimated 70 individuals.

Revegetation of the Styles Creek covenant area in Broad Bay, an on-going project of Save The Otago Peninsula Inc, should help this gecko to extend its range.

Left: *A Jewelled gecko, marked with blue spots by scientists studying its movements, basks on a* Coprosma propinqua *bush.*

Right: *Map of the Otago Peninsula showing places mentioned in this chapter.*

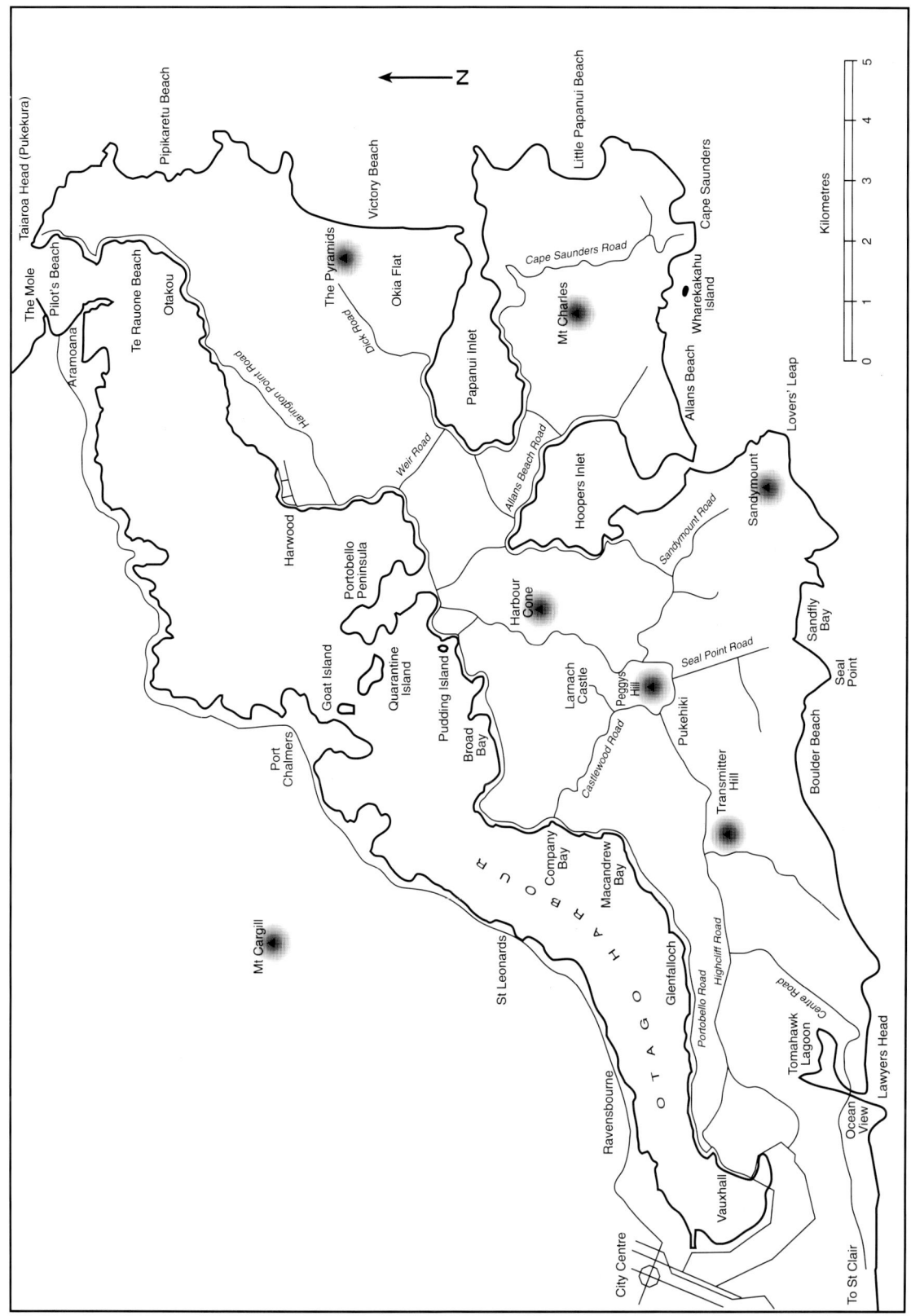

Island life. Top to bottom: Sooty shearwaters or Titi in flight, Royal spoonbill in Taupata canopy, Little shag and nestling, Stewart Island shag and nestling, Blue penguin.

Chris Gaskin

Chapter 4   ISLANDS Aloof havens

Islands are intriguing places. They conjure up thoughts of remoteness, tranquillity, and nature unspoiled. Most people – certainly those for whom wilderness is a tonic – feel compelled to explore islands where they can. Around Dunedin, however, the opportunities are few. Lake Wanaka holds as many islands of note as the Dunedin coastline.

Nonetheless, each of the Dunedin islands retains unique natural or conservation values of one kind or another. In common with other New Zealand regions, Dunedin has islands that are important havens for rare or special fauna and flora.

A map showing the locations of islands and estuaries in the Dunedin area appears on page 57.

The offshore islands are Green Island or Okaihae off the Waldronville coast, White Island or Pounuiahine off St Clair Beach, and Wharekakahu, which lies between Cape Saunders and Allans Beach. Taieri Island or Moturata, guarding the mouth of the Taieri River, can be reached on foot at low tide.

Otago Harbour has two 'halfway' islands – Quarantine Island or Kamautaurua (also known as St Martin Island) and Goat Island or Rangiriri – which all but span the gap between Port Chalmers and Portobello Peninsula. Nearer Portobello village is tiny circular Pudding Island or Titeremoana, a scenic reserve entirely covered in low forest to the cliff edge, in the way the harbour shores were clothed in pre-European times.

Below: *Green Island from the southern side, with Kaikorai Estuary in the distance. The tiny white dots in the canopy at the centre of the photograph are Royal spoonbills. Their main nesting area, however, is at the right (eastern) end.*

Finally, and in a different category again, is Rabbit Island, which stands out – just – above the tidal flats of Blueskin Bay.

Neville Peat

Left: Hebe elliptica *flowering in a typical cliff-face situation.*

GREEN ISLAND Treasure Island

Volcanic Green Island, 4.5ha in extent, 42m high and 2.2km from the mainland, is a natural treasure. A nature reserve (closed to the public; landings by permit only), it is chock-a-block with seabirds.

The Blue penguin population alone is impressive, although it fluctuates a lot. Nest counts can range from 100 to 1,500, depending on factors such as food supply. Yellow-eyed penguins or Hoiho are rather more consistent – 25-30 pairs. Stewart Island shags nest in a tight colony on open ground on the north face (100-200 nests), and Royal spoonbills or Kotuku-ngutupapa in recent years have established a colony of about 30 nests in the canopy of the predominant shrub, *Coprosma repens* or Taupata. Little shags also nest in the canopy.

Fairy prions or Titi-wainui, a small blue-grey petrel about half the size of the Sooty shearwater, are abundant (in the order of 1,000 nests). They nest in burrows, on crevices or in caves. They also have a small colony on the sandstone cliffs near Tunnel Beach, which suggests they might have nested in greater numbers on the mainland in the past, but succumbed to predators. These prions breed on offshore islands in many parts of New Zealand, as well as on numerous subantarctic islands around the Southern Ocean.

Southern Black-backed gulls find Green Island conducive. Their nests number about 200 each year. Only a handful of Sooty shearwaters nest here, though. Variable (Black) oystercatchers – two or three pairs – breed on the island, nesting close to the water.

One of the most remarkable features of the birdlife of Green Island involves an introduced species – Starling. In their thousands, Starlings flock to the island from the mainland on a daily basis, around dusk, to roost in the Taupata

The pinkish-purple larvae of the geometrid moth Pasiphila charybdis *feed on the leaves of the Coastal speedwell* Hebe elliptica. *Dunedin is the type locality for the moth species, whose close relative P. fumipalpata feeds on the flowers of this shrub, which supports many insects.*

Royal Newcomers

Royal spoonbills or Kotukungutupapa *Platalea regia* nest in bushes of Taupata *Coprosma repens* on Green Island – the southernmost colony in New Zealand. Breeding was confirmed in 1988, and by 1995 the colony had built up to 25 nests.

There is another colony at Maukiekie Island off Moeraki Peninsula, established in 1984. Royal spoonbills also breed near Okarito Lagoon and at Wairau Lagoon in Marlborough. Although the two Otago colonies are younger, Otago is now the New Zealand Royal spoonbill capital. Over 200 birds were sighted between Kakanui and Catlins Lake during a census in February 1995.

Like the distantly-related White heron or Kotuku, Royal spoonbills are self-introduced from Australia. They feed on tidal mud flats in a distinctive way, sweeping their extraordinary jet-black spoon-shaped bills from side to side in search of small fish and estuarine crustaceans, molluscs and worms.

Kaikorai Estuary is a favourite haunt, and they are often seen from the bridge on Brighton Road. They can appear at any of the Dunedin estuaries and even on mud flats on Otago Harbour. At Green Island the breeding season begins in October, with the return of the birds from winter quarters in northern areas of New Zealand. Nests are built of sticks and leaves and one to four eggs are laid. The chicks fledge in about seven weeks, after which they follow and are fed by their parents for a few weeks.

Right: *Spoonbill chick and eggs, Green Island. Roosting nearby is a Little shag.*

canopy overnight. Only a few breed there, however.

There is a healthy population of Common gecko *Heterophilus maculatus* on Green Island.

Shrubland covers about 40 percent of the island, the rest being rocky or covered in herbs or bird droppings. The guano inhibits all but a few plants.

Green Island has a small flora compared to the harbour islands – just eight native species and ten naturalised ones. Taupata, a native shrub, dominates the scene. Its shiny foliage forms virtually the whole canopy, which reaches about 4m in height in sheltered places but is characteristically 1-2m. The only other shrub species here is *Hebe elliptica*, which once predominated. There are only a few Hebe trees left now. Since about 1960 the Hebe has been all but displaced by Taupata – an astonishing transformation. Underneath the Taupata, the ground is largely bare except for leaf litter.

Taupata proliferates on the Dunedin coastline, although its natural southern limit is thought to be Kaikoura. It may have been brought south as a hedging plant. In Australia it is known as New Zealand mirror bush and regarded as a weed. At Phillip Island near Melbourne, a Blue penguin stronghold, attempts have been made to eradicate it.

A handful of plants of the rare and endangered Cooks scurvy grass *Lepidium oleraceum* grow on the south side of the island on two sites. Muddy terraces on the west side are covered by mats of the fleshy herb *Crassula moschata* and the common introduced grass *Poa annua*. Other exotic plant species on Green Island include the tall tree mallow *Lavatera arborea*, which is being controlled.

Neville Peat

QUARANTINE & GOAT ISLANDS Species rich

The two islands that divide Otago Harbour into Upper and Lower compartments – Quarantine Kamautaurua and Goat Rangiriri – retain a diverse array of plant life, with each island boasting about 100 native species.

On Quarantine Island (14ha, 58m above sea level at summit), dense native forest covers western areas, which are fenced off from pasture grazed by sheep. Hall's totara, Mahoe, Broadleaf, Ngaio and Kohuhu make up the bulk of the canopy. What impresses in this low forest is the proliferation of climbing plants or lianes – 11 species all told. They add complexity to the forest. It becomes a jungle.

With no possums on the island to eat their leaves and flowers, the lianes can scramble at will. Climbing anise *Scandia geniculata*, which is palatable to stock and now fairly rare in the Dunedin area, is well established on Quarantine Island. So too is the native bindweed *Calystegia tuguriorum*, which is similar to garden convolvulus but with smaller flowers (up to 5cm diameter) and distinctive orange seeds. White-flowered Climbing rata *Metrosideros diffusa* and the native Jasmine *Parsonsia heterophylla* are abundant. Ferns dominate the ground cover.

Southern black-backed gull chick close to its nest on a rock stack beside Pudding Island Titeremoana near Portobello. The island is fully covered by a dense forest of Ngaio, Kohuhu, Broadleaf and Totara that reaches a surprising height – 7m.

Left: *Wind-shorn shrubs and trees on the south side of Quarantine Island –* Peppertree *(foreground), small-leaved* Coprosma *species hosting the mistletoe* Ileostylus micranthus, *and Hall's totara.*

Right: *This white-fronted tern was defending a nest site below iceplant flowers on the cliffs of Pudding Island. These cliffs provide habitat for three micro-casemoth species.*

Above: *Flax flowers (January) rise above mixed shrubland on the south-west side of Quarantine Island. In the distance is Harbour Cone.*

The forest is in much better condition overall than similar forest on adjacent Otago Peninsula. The island, separated from the Peninsula by a 100m-wide channel swept by tidal currents, is free not only of possums but also of rabbits, cats, mice, stoats and ferrets – good news for the Bellbird, Grey warbler and other bush birds. Rats are present but under control. Southern Black-backed gulls nest on grassy slopes close to the water and Little shags build their nests in trees at the water's edge or overhanging it. Sheep have grazed the island for decades, but are being reduced gradually. At the same time, planting out of native trees and shrubs by the Conservation Corps, Kiwi Conservation Club (Forest and Bird), Dunedin Amenities Society and St Martin Island Community is assisting natural revegetation.

In summer, the air around the forest margins is alive with butterflies – Red Admiral, Tussock and two Copper species (Common and Glade).

Quarantine Island is a recreation reserve managed by the Department of Conservation and leased to the St Martin Island Community. Visitors are welcome. From 1863 to the 1920s, the island was a quarantine station. Passengers from 41 immigrant vessels were quarantined there. A cemetery surrounded by a relatively new picket fence recalls the fact that some 72 immigrants died of diseases. The introduced conifers, including Scots pine around the cemetery, date from the quarantine station era. World War I soldiers suffering venereal disease were housed in the island's hospital. In 1928, huskies with Admiral Richard Evelyn Byrd's Antarctic expedition were quarantined on the island. Lacking fresh water, the island was never the site of major settlement by early Maori.

The main shipping channel separates Quarantine Island from Goat Island Rangiriri, a scenic reserve (4.6ha, 40m above sea level), where regenerating low forest covers virtually the whole island. Cleared of its original forest in the 1870s for quarantine purposes, Goat Island now bears an outstanding example of the Ngaio-Kohuhu association. Cabbage trees *Cordyline australis* (Ti), Totara and an occasional Miro are emergent. In addition to having most of the climbing plants found on Quarantine, Goat Island has Supplejack or Kareao *Ripogonum scandens*. It, too, is free of introduced browsing animals.

Above: *Cliff-bound* **Wharekakahu Island** *(2.1ha, 52m high), a nature reserve off-limits to the public, is separated from the Otago Peninsula coastline by about 300m of often-stormy ocean. Cape Saunders Light is about 1km away. As on Green Island, Fairy prions and Stewart Island shags breed in number here,with about 200 shag nests. Spotted shags, which do not breed on Green Island, presumably because of the lack of cliff nesting habitat, build 20 to 50 nests per year on Wharekakahu.*

Another seabird absent from Green Island, the Red-billed gull, also breeds on Wharekakahu. Two lizards are here: the Common gecko Hoplodactylus maculatus *and Green skink* Leiolopisma chloronoton. *The former is found throughout New Zealand, the latter (growing to a length of 20cm) only in Otago, Southland and Stewart Island. A key element of the vegetation is the small blue shore tussock* Poa astonii, *but colonisation by Stewart Island shags has reduced its extent.*

Above: *Three species of microcasemoth are found on the islands and coast of Dunedin. Pictured is the male of one of two undescribed* Reductoderces *species, which reaches its northern limit on Otago Peninsula and its islands. Wingless females cling to their cases after emerging on calm frosty mornings in July-August, then release a distinctive scent (pheromone) to attract a mate. They lay their eggs back in the empty case. The cases are small but can occur in very large numbers. The larvae carry around the case for shelter and camouflage as they feed on various algae species. The third species* Scoriodyta patricki *is found from Oamaru south to Otago Peninsula, with Portobello being the type locality.*

Titeremoana Restored

Titeremoana (0.8ha) is a scenic reserve which can be reached on foot. In December 1909 careless visitors caused a fire which partly destroyed the indigenous vegetation. The following year the island was declared a reserve and replanted with native species by the Forest Service. This accounts for the presence on the island of some odd trees – Akiraho *Olearia paniculata*, which does not occur naturally south of Oamaru but is common as a hedge around Dunedin, and silver beech *Nothofagus menziesii*, rare at sea level in the Dunedin region. The three pohutukawa *Metrosideros excelsa* which grow on the eastern side of the island and flower in January-February (later than northern trees), probably date from this early exercise in habitat restoration, which saw the planting of over 900 seedlings. Today the understorey over much of the island is relatively open, with Hound's tongue fern *Phymatosorus diversifolius* and tangled native Jasmine providing a fairly complete ground cover.

MOTURATA Titi territory

Moturata or Taieri Island (an elongate 6.8ha, 31m at its highest point) is joined to the mainland by a sand bar that is covered at high tide. As a result of a history of human occupation and use – initially by local Maori, then by European whalers – its vegetation is much modified.

Flax *Phormium tenax* dominates. Other notable native species are Bracken *Pteridium esculentum*, Silver tussock *Poa cita* and Poroporo *Solanum laciniatum*. Native celery *Apium prostratum*, not unlike flat-leaved parsley in appearance, grows just above the high-tide mark. Like the cress *Lepidium oleraceum*, it was used by Captain Cook to ward off scurvy. Gorse and thistles are scattered across the island's grassy slopes.

A revegetation programme involving members of the Moturata-Taieri Mouth Whanau and other residents, working in conjunction with the Department of Conservation, is expected to restore shrubland on northern parts of the island. Rabbits have inhabited the island in the past and will be a threat to regeneration if not controlled.

Rabbits in number would compete for burrowing space with Titi (Sooty shearwaters), whose presence on the island is of significance to Maori people. Harvesting of Titi chicks as muttonbirds is still a traditional practice of southern Maori on islands around Stewart Island, but it is not permitted on Moturata, a scenic reserve. In spring, Titi migrate south in their millions from winter quarters in the North Pacific. Huge flocks work their way south along the Dunedin coast. They crowd on to islands in southern New Zealand, especially in the Stewart Island and Foveaux Strait

Rod Morris

Right: *Sooty shearwater or Titi* Puffinus griseus.

area and at The Snares, raising a single chick per pair over summer. Smaller colonies are located on the mainland and on islands such as Green and Moturata. The chicks are ready to fledge in April/May, after which they join the adults in the long migration flight north.

The island's name, literally Rata Island, may reflect the presence of Southern rata *Metrosideros umbellata* at one time. Rata does not occur naturally in the Dunedin area. It extends north along the coast from South Otago as far as Akatore, close to Taieri Mouth. Its absence north of here is a mystery.

Left: *Rabbit Island inhabitant –* Coprosma acerosa *fruiting.*

RABBIT ISLAND Low profile

Rabbit Island, about 1km long and rising only a few metres above sea level, is surrounded by the saltmarsh of Blueskin Bay. The saltmarsh (see Chapter 5) has not been disturbed much, but vegetation on the island proper has suffered by the invasion of gorse, broom and *Pinus radiata*. Manuka *Leptospermum scoparium* is holding its own, however, at the north and south ends of the island, with some trees growing to 6m. The Sand Coprosma *Coprosma acerosa* has been recorded on the island. Reaching 2m, it produces translucent pale-blue fruit in late summer.

Right: *Map showing locations of islands and estuaries in the Dunedin area.*

Night Moth

The noctuid moth *Agrotis innominata* has larvae feeding on both Marram grass and Sand convolvulus *Calystegia soldanella*. While the males are strong fliers, the females in Otago populations are brachypterous and consequently flightless, which greatly limits the dispersal ability of the species. Pictured is the flightless adult female.

The Katipo spider *Lactrodectus katipo*, which lives exclusively in sandy areas and always near the sea, is at its southern limit at Doctors Point. The only poisonous animal native to New Zealand, it belongs to a group of poisonous spiders found in many parts of the world.

Only the female is able to bite. She is shiny black with a red-striped abdomen the size of a garden pea, and like many other spiders, she guards her eggsac to prevent other creatures, notably carnivorous beetles, from eating them. Females may live 18 to 24 months but males are short-lived (5-6 weeks). The male is quite different – much smaller with a white abdomen that carries black bands and light-red or orange diamonds.

Shy spiders, Katipo are far less dangerous than their reputation suggests. Sometimes they are caught up in driftwood collected from the beach. They live in marram grass and other seashore vegetation, although may shelter under empty cans or other rubbish. Their Maori name means 'night biter'.

R.R. Forster

Chapter 5 ESTUARIES, INLETS AND LAGOONS
Caressed by the tide

Islands stand fast against the tide; estuaries, inlets and lagoons have a rather more accommodating relationship with the sea. Caressed by tides twice a day, they are among the most dynamic places in nature, not to mention the most seminal. Long before dinosaurs ruled the earth, marine fauna with terrestrial ambitions slithered ashore in the shelter and repose of estuaries – and gained a foothold. Among the habitats of the modern world, estuaries remain the creative enginerooms of nature they once were. For an object lesson in the rhythms and interconnectedness of nature, look no further than an estuary.

What Dunedin lacks in the way of islands it makes up for in tidal inlets, estuaries and lagoons. The list includes (north to south) Hawksbury Lagoon, Waikouaiti River Estuary at Karitane/Merton, Blueskin Bay and Orokonui Inlets, Purakanui Inlet, Aramoana, Hoopers and Papanui Inlets on Otago Peninsula, Tomahawk Lagoon, Kaikorai Estuary and Lagoon, and Taieri Mouth. Estuaries typically are river mouths defined by a sand spit behind which the tide covers and uncovers an expanse of mudflats and saltmarsh. Otago Harbour, strictly speaking, is an inlet but it resembles a broad river in shape, complete with a sand spit that protects a splendid estuary – Aramoana.

Saltmarsh can be divided into zones (commonly upper, middle and lower), with the size and make-up of each zone determined by the extent to which it is immersed and exposed by the tide and the degree of salinity in the sandy soils. The upper marsh is flooded only at spring tides, which occur with each full and new moon. Behind the marsh there are often sand ridges and wet slacks, which together act as a giant filter. Freshwater run-off is intercepted and mixed gradually with the brine, providing plants with some assurance of salinity levels. As sea levels rise and fall over eons, the saltmarsh migrates, retaining its pattern of zonation.

The productivity of estuaries – the intertidal flats and saltmarsh – is astonishing. New Zealand studies suggest estuaries may produce as much as 2000g of plant matter per square metre a year (compared to 730g for land and 155g for the ocean). At least 30 commercially important fish species, including flounder, mullet, sole, gurnard, red cod, eels and whitebait, migrate through estuaries.

This huge productivity is possible because, twice a day, the tide freshens the nutrient supply. For the micro-organisms, plants, shellfish, crustaceans, fish and birds it is a regular, moving feast. The tide also brings in sediment, which shifts about, building here, eroding there, steadily redefining the shape of things in an estuary.

A map showing the locations of estuaries, inlets, lagoons and islands in the Dunedin area appears on page 57.

Left: *Estuary birds. From foreground: Eastern Bar-tailed godwit or Kuaka, Banded dotterel or Tuturiwhatu, Australasian Pied stilt or Poaka.*

Some 800,000 tonnes of sediment pours into Otago Harbour over a year. Some of this exits with the ebb tide, but much of it settles. Without dredging (and if sea levels remained the same), the harbour would fill up in about 150 years. At low tide about 30 percent of the harbour (4,600ha) is exposed as flats. It takes only two tides to turn over water in the lower harbour but 27 tides (just on two weeks) for a complete turnover to be achieved in the upper harbour, separated from the lower compartment by the two islands near Port Chalmers.

Catalogue of Misuse

In Dunedin as elsewhere in New Zealand, estuaries and the shallows of inlets and lagoons used to be regarded by Europeans as being muddy eyesores – wastelands in limbo, of value only when reclaimed and put to human use.

The poor image of estuaries is no better expressed than in the siting of public rubbish dumps on many of them – a crude and contaminating form of reclamation. There have been other uses – plantation forestry, sports grounds, causeway roading, subdivisions. Only in recent times has the ecological importance of estuaries been recognised, including their role as nursery areas for fish and as sources of enrichment for coastal waters.

Reclamation has a habit of creeping up on and severely modifying an estuarine ecosystem. In Otago Harbour, the total area reclaimed since 1847 is now close to 400ha – 8 percent of the original area at high water. The upper harbour is practically devoid of estuarine habitat. An area of about 25ha centred on Logan Park was once a sizeable wetland – Lake Logan. Much of the commercial and industrial sector of downtown Dunedin occupies reclaimed mudflats and saltmarsh.

The estuary of the Waikouaiti River had by far the greatest area of pre-European saltmarsh in Otago. The bulk of it was drained for farmland.

In 1994 a proposal for a significant new reclamation at Deborah Bay received initial planning approval. Together with reclamations to do with port development at Port Chalmers, the Deborah Bay proposal marks a renewal of interest in reclaiming areas of the harbour.

Aramoana saltmarsh is now protected within the network of reserves managed by the Department of Conservation, but for many years it was threatened by industrial development. In 1972, the Aramoana saltmarsh and mudflats were earmarked as the site of an aluminium smelter, and in 1981 a second and much larger proposal was mooted – similar in size to Southland's Tiwai Point plant.

A vociferous public campaign opposed the scheme, which was eventually abandoned as uneconomic. The Department of Conservation now manages 120ha of saltmarsh and an adjacent buffer zone as an ecological area. A further 250ha of intertidal flats is also protected.

Above: *Glasswort* Sarcocornia quinqueflora *at Aramoana, with Saltmarsh ribbonwood in the background. Glasswort also grows on hard shores and cliffs near the sea. Its common name relates to the use of the plant's mineral-rich ash in an old glassmaking process.*

Caterpillars thrive on this plant, notably those of the moth Ectopatria aspera, *which are initially green and closely resemble the foliage of glasswort. When the caterpillars become too large to be camouflaged effectively, they turn brown and grey, with rows of white spots dorsally, and hide amongst the stems and litter at the base of the plant.*

ARAMOANA Showpiece saltmarsh

The saltmarsh tucked in behind Aramoana Spit is the largest and most intact saltmarsh in the Dunedin region and one of the best examples left on the South Island's east coast.

Fully protected now, the saltmarsh contains a representative suite of plants. Some enjoy a dip in the sea on a daily basis and some only occasionally. Others are shy of the water but accept a shake of salt around their roots. Here the tidal range at mean springs is 1.65m (at Dunedin, 22km from here, the range is 1.8m).

Saltmarsh plants that withstand regular submergence at high tide are a select group. They include Glasswort *Sarcocornia quinqueflora*, a succulent whose jointed stems form dense mats. The stems range in colour from reddish brown to blue-green. The Sedge three-square *Schoenoplectus pungens*, which grows in open clumps, is also to be found at the reception centre for the incoming tide. It is an old salt of the plant world, having crossed many seas to establish in Europe and North and South America as well as in Australia and New Zealand.

In the middle marsh, submerged for less time, are turf-forming Remuremu *Selliera radicans* and Shore pimpernel or Maakoako *Samolus repens*. They look alike, these two

Selliera radicans *or Remuremu in flower, Otago Harbour.*

ground-huggers, but their flowers are distinguishing. Samolus bears white stars; Selliera's white flowers seem lopsided, with a petal or two missing. Both plants are found in Australia. Samolus's range extends to Easter Island. Associated plants in the middle zone are *Suaeda novae-zelandiae*, a reddish endemic sea blite, and the purple-flowered saltmarsh musk *Mimulus repens*. Other distinctive marsh species are Bachelor's button *Cotula coronopifolia*, whose yellow flowers are bright as the proverbial button, and *Lilaeopsis novae-zelandiae*, a South Island endemic (type locality, Tomahawk Lagoon) whose cylindrical leaves arise from creeping rhizomes. These and other plants form meadows whose upper boundary is marked by plants of distinctly higher stature.

In the upper saltmarsh are found tall rushes and sedges. Prominent is Jointed rush or Oioi *Leptocarpus similis*, which grows in dense stands to over 1m tall with foliage delicately and diversely coloured – blue-green, grey, orange, purple. Marsh ribbonwood *Plagianthus divaricatus* is often associated with jointed rush – the only shrub (reaching over 2m) to tolerate the saline conditions of the upper saltmarsh and one of New Zealand's few native deciduous species. At Aramoana and other places, the ribbonwood associates with New Zealand flax or Harakeke *Phormium tenax*.

From the ribbonwood to the Selliera, marsh plants provide food for over 80 native moth species. Other notable insects include several native Staphylinid beetles and a large native Chafer *Pericoptus truncatus*, which is found in the dunes adjacent to the marsh. The jointed rush/ribbonwood area is habitat, too, for Fernbird *Bowdleria punctata*, a vulnerable native species.

The sand ridges extending inland, reaching 7m above mean sea level, probably originated between 4,000 and

Problem Plants

♦ An Asian seaweed *Undaria pinnatifida*, which thrives in sheltered waters, is becoming a threat to native marine plants. It was discovered at Port Chalmers and the Dunedin Steamer Basin in 1990. Introduced accidentally with water ballast discharged by overseas ships, Undaria may locally displace the ubiquitous native bladder kelp *Macrocystis pyrifera* if left unchecked. In Asia, the seaweed is farmed as Wakami.

♦ The cord grass *Spartina anglica*, introduced from Britain to assist reclamation of estuaries, is capable of destroying native saltmarsh vegetation if not kept in check. It is an aggressive plant, forming stout clumps to knee height and spreading rhizomes through tidal mud. By trapping sediments it can elevate a tidal zone. Spartina had a foothold at Merton near Cherry Farm in the 1980s but has been controlled by a spraying programme undertaken by the Department of Conservation.

Above: *Kaikorai Estuary and Lagoon*, located near the suburb of Green Island, suffered the mindless abuse of industrial pollution and contamination from rubbish dumps for many years. In the new era of sanitary landfills and pollution awareness there is hope the estuary can be restored to its full natural potential as a habitat and feeding ground for seabirds and water birds.

The Dunedin City Council is making improvements at its Green Island landfill and is restoring wetland habitat. Pukeko are increasing in number. Perhaps Bittern, Marsh crake and Fernbird will return to the restored shrubland, and migratory Caspian terns will take up breeding on marsh islands nearer the sea. The area has established populations of Mallard and Grey Duck and New Zealand Shoveler. A total of 30 bird species has been recorded at Kaikorai Estuary. In the distance is Green Island.

6,000 years ago, when sea levels were about 2m above present levels.

Since the erection of the Mole (official name, Cargill Pier) in the 1880s, the Spit has been seriously eroded. It used to be much broader. About 12ha has been lost. The saltmarsh, however, owes much to the erection of the Mole, because it extinguished a second channel to the sea and allowed the sandy flats once occupying the site to be invaded by saltmarsh vegetation.

Fringing the Aramoana saltmarsh on the harbour side are intertidal flats that extend for 3km from the end of the Spit to Otafelo Point. Snails and crabs mark the exposed shiny mud with wiggly lines, and the thin dark leaves of Seagrass or eelgrass *Zostera novazelandica*, erect and waving when covered in water, lie flat as if exhausted when the tide is out.

On flats clear of vegetation the most common shellfish is the New Zealand cockle *Austrovenus stutchburyi* (more properly a clam but called a cockle by Captain Cook, who thought them the same as Thames Estuary cockles). Filter-feeders, cockles achieve an unbelievable density at stable sites where the supply of planktonic food is at an optimum. In tightly packed beds, they can number in the order of several thousand per square metre. A total weight of over

Neville Peat

Left: Red-billed gulls feeding on a stranding of red lobster krill Munida gregaria *at Portobello. In summer, dense swarms enter the harbour and strand on beaches right up to the head of the harbour. They provide easy pickings for gulls, either in the water or on beaches uncovered by the tide.* Munida *is a galatheid crab and the krill, known also as whalefeed, a postlarval form. 'White krill'* Nyctiphanes australis *is also seasonally conspicuous in the harbour.*

30kg per square metre has been recorded. Such is their number, dead cockle shells wash ashore to form whole beaches.

Other molluscs roam the intertidal area. Topshells rasp microscopic algae from Zostera leaves. Whelks are carnivorous. They prey on cockles and other shellfish by boring directly through the shell. Unrelated to bivalves such as cockles are two species of brachiopods – shellfish of ancient lineage. In all, 400 species of seabed invertebrate animals have been recorded from Otago Harbour.

Ninety species of fish are known from the harbour, with the Aramoana area playing a key role as a juvenile rearing habitat.

Little wonder then, that at low tide the mudflats and nearby shallow waters throng with seabirds and wading birds that come to prey on shellfish, finfish, crustaceans and worms. Pied oystercatchers, Banded dotterels and Red-billed and Southern Black-backed gulls all take part in the feast, and in the summer they are joined by migratory birds, notably Eastern Bar-tailed godwits. The waders include White-faced herons, Pied stilts and on occasion, Royal spoonbills and White herons.

Most birds follow the edge of the ebbing tide, exploring the flats on foot as they become exposed. Black swans, which graze the seagrass, operate the other way. They would rather float than waddle on foot to reach the seagrass, so they swim with the floodtide, dipping their long necks to pull at the grass under water.

The droppings of all these birds contribute substantially to the nutrient soup of the intertidal flats and saltmarsh.

Tidal meadows

Seagrass *Zostera novazelandica*, spending half its life submerged, is more than a food for black swans and vegetarian shellfish. It creates microhabitats amongst its dense roots and leaves. It also traps sand and shell gravel and forms habitat for juvenile fish.

Seagrass will establish only where the salinity is not too low and where the intertidal flats are gently graded. The tidal current cannot be too strong or the plant will scour out; nor can it be too weak or it will become smothered in silt. Its tiny flowers are fertilised under water and rarely seen.

The roots go deep into the rich black mud that typically underlies seagrass – mud enriched by generations of decaying organisms and plants, including seagrass. Seagrass is an important source of phosphorus in the estuarine system.

George Chance

Above: *A Black swan nesting in Raupo. Besides that at Hawksbury Lagoon, there are populations of Black swans at Blueskin Bay, Tomahawk, Hoopers and Papanui Inlets, Kaikorai, and Waihola.*

Black Swans

The population of Black swans *Cygnus atratus* at Hawksbury Lagoon, Waikouaiti, has been a hallmark of the area in the past. In 1993, however, the population crashed from 300-400 to just 10 – a phenomenon that was linked to an algal bloom in the shallow waters of the lagoon, caused by nutrient enrichment or eutrophication. The reduced transparency resulted in a marked decline in the bottom-dwelling algae upon which the swans fed, thus the swans moved away. Something similar happened in 1985.

Black swans are no longer regarded as an introduced species *per se*. Numbers of them were imported from Australia in the 1860s as a game bird and liberated in Otago as well as other parts of the South Island, but no one could account for the population suddenly swelling in the 1960s. Today ornithologists accept there must have been self-introductions then and at later periods.

Black swans do not breed every year. No more than a third of birds in a breeding area in any one year will attempt to nest. Usually five or six eggs are incubated, within 24 hours of hatching, the cygnets are led to water. Before their breeding years young swans may fly to other regions. The Otago coast sometimes receives visits from Canterbury birds. Black swans are vegetarians, eating mainly aquatic plants. Hawksbury Lagoon is a 61ha wildlife management reserve whose reserve status dates from 1900, when it was recognised as an important refuge for 'native and imported game'. Shooting is not permitted. Public access is maintained.

Right: *Bladder kelp* Macrocystis pyrifera, *distinguished by its floats or bladders and ribbon-like form, is common along rocky shores in Otago Harbour and the Dunedin inlets. Although mainly a subtidal seaweed growing up to 20m long, it is sometimes seen bunched up in the shallows at low tide. In deeper water its upper leaves collect at the surface, forming a brown belt parallel to the shore. Bladder kelp is reputed to be the world's fastest-growing plant. Leaves can put on half a metre a day. Widely distributed, it is harvested in California as a source of alginic acid by barges that mow the top 2m with each harvest.*

Left: *Bull kelp* Durvillaea antarctica *swirls with pink sea tulips, an intertidal animal, in a rock pool at Murdering Beach (Whareakeake). The bulkiest New Zealand seaweed, inhabiting rocky shores where it can gain an anchorage, Bull kelp produces fronds up to 10m long. The holdfast anchoring individual plants is undermined by shellfish and worms, often causing the plant to break away and wash ashore.*

A closely related kelp, Durvillaea willana, *grows to 5m and is distinguished by its more tree-like form. Its blades lack the internal buoyant honeycomb tissue of* D. antarctica. *It is generally located below the zone of Bull kelp and is not attacked by burrowing animals.*

Sea tulips, attached by stalks up to 1m long, belong to an order of marine animals called acidians or sea squirts. They feed by taking in water through siphons. Sea tulips Pyura pachydermatina *are plentiful along rocky shores of Otago Harbour and adjacent coast.*

PENINSULA INLETS A godwit haven

Hoopers and Papanui Inlets on the ocean side of Otago Peninsula are bountiful for birds.

At Papanui (350ha), 44 species have been recorded, 24 of them regular users. Among the more unusual visitors is Glossy ibis, which wanders to New Zealand from Australia but has not begun breeding here yet. It belongs to the same family as Royal spoonbill. Besides a regular array of seabirds, Papanui and Hoopers Inlets attract Australasian harrier (Kahu), New Zealand kingfisher (Kotare), Paradise shelduck (Putakitaki) and Spur-winged plover.

A regular user in late spring and summer is the Eastern Bar-tailed godwit or Kuaka *Limosa lapponica baueri*, which migrates to Australasia from breeding grounds in Siberia and northern Alaska. Flocks of 2,000 godwits are not uncommon on the Peninsula inlets at low tide, busily probing the mud and sand with their long, slightly upturned bills. Godwits often search for molluscs, crustaceans and worms in the company of South Island Pied oystercatchers, but are easily distinguished from the black-and-white oystercatchers by their mottled brown plumage.

Among shellfish populations, cockles and pipi are abundant. At Papanui there has been commercial harvesting of cockles, which are marketed as clams, for a number of years. Both inlets hold communities of crabs, notably the stalk-eyed mud crab, and burrowing anemones, and both are important nurseries for Sand and Green-back flounders.

Periodically, the entrance at Hoopers Inlet (380ha) is blocked with sand. In 1993, a large landslip occurred at the Sandymount Wildlife Refuge adjacent to the entrance. Tidal access was blocked for months.

The saltmarsh around both inlets has been largely modified by roading or farmland development. At Hoopers Inlet, patches of Copper tussock *Chionochloa rubra cuprea* grow behind surviving saltmarsh – a feature not found at Aramoana. At Papanui, peat outcrops on the southern fringe indicate that Silver beech forest grew here between glaciations over 20,000 years ago.

A study of the animal life in the saltmarsh and salt meadow of Hoopers Inlet in the 1950s demonstrated the immense productivity of such habitats. At its maximum the microfauna (including amphipods, copepods, tardigrades, rotifers and nematodes) numbered 7.5 million animals per square metre.

Neville Peat

Left: *The Rock crab* Hemigrapsus edwardsii *is common on sheltered shores in the mid-tide zone, and is especially abundant in Otago Harbour. When threatened, it will rock back on its hind legs and wave its claws menacingly. Its square back is purple and cream and can measure 50 mm across. By day it hides under rocks when the tide is out and like many crabs scavenges for food and is preyed upon by octopuses and fish. Also common but inhabiting sandy shores in the subtidal zone is the Paddle crab* Ovalipes catharus, *whose large pinkish shell (up to saucer size) is often found washed up on beaches. This crab has paddle-shaped back legs which it uses for swimming and also for burying itself into the sand.*

OROKONUI INLET A fishy story

Orokonui Inlet, which feeds into the much larger Blueskin Bay Inlet, and its freshwater source, Orokonui Stream, are remarkable for their native fish populations. No fewer than nine species have been recorded here – three galaxiids, three bullies, two eels and a lamprey.

Consequently, the area is prime habitat for New Zealand kingfishers. A tree planting programme along the banks of the stream, undertaken by school children as a conservation project, is enhancing the habitat.

Upstream, an old plantation of Eucalypts features one tree that has become a tourist attraction because of its designation as New Zealand's tallest tree – a 69m-high mountain ash *Eucalyptus regnans*. A wild population of Eastern rosellas, birds introduced from Australia, seems right at home here.

Above: *A surprising find on saltmarsh on the west side of Rabbit Island in 1989 was the day-flying moth* Eurythecta leucothrinca, *whose recognised habitat is grassland in upland areas of Otago. The female of the species is flightless. It is thought to be present at sea level because the rocks of the Dunedin volcano depressed the eastern edge of the old Otago peneplain to sea level and below.*

Accessible from Waitati, the Orokonui Inlet saltmarsh has prominent stands of Jointed rush *Leptocarpus similis* in association with the Sedges *Isolepis marginata* and three-square *Schoenoplectus pungens*, and expanses of Bachelor's button *Cotula coronopifolia*.

Near Waitati in Blueskin Bay there is a good example of saltmarsh grading into coastal shrubland remnants containing *Coprosma* species, Ngaio, Manuka and Hall's totara. Across the inlet at Rabbit Island there is an excellent sequence of marsh grading into Saltmarsh ribbonwood, New Zealand flax and Silver tussock.

Estuary insects

Saltmarsh insect life is surprisingly diverse, considering the relatively small extent of the habitat. Aramoana has over 80 moth species.

A high percentage of insects are diurnal. Many of the moths are day-flying, notably *Eutorna symmorpha*, whose larvae mine Selliera leaves, and *Arctesthes catapyrrha*, whose larvae are found on *Plantago* here.

Saltmarsh ribbonwood is the exclusive host of a small moth *Stigmella aigialeia*. One leaf will feed its leaf-mining caterpillar for a lifetime. At the other end of the scale is a geometrid moth *Pseudocoremia lactiflua*, whose looper larvae are capable of devouring many ribbonwood leaves.

Chapter 6 FORESTS Tall survivors

Two hundred years ago coastal Dunedin was a forested land of plenty. Dense forest and shrubland covered the land from sea level to the sub-alpine zone. Trees overhung harbour waters. Kaka filled the canopy with their melodious parrot calls. Mohua (Yellowhead) added canary colour and charming song. Brown kiwi were recorded calling as late as 1873, although there is some doubt about this record.

The bulk of the original forest cover disappeared in the latter half of the nineteenth century following the arrival of European settlers, who felled the impressive podocarps, mainly Rimu, Miro, Kahikatea, Matai and Totara, for building timber. Lowland forest occupied land that was required for farming, so it had to go. The least promising patches survived. They include higher forest and the more remote patches. Today, they combine with regenerating shrubland to give the city – the hilly eastern parts anyway – a reasonably leafy countenance. Plantation forests of *Pinus radiata* and Douglas fir have been imposed on the landscape – geometric and uniformly dark-green.

Around metropolitan Dunedin the forest would have been dominated by tall podocarp trees. In the subcanopy we can picture such medium-sized trees as Lemonwood or Tarata *Pittosporum eugenioides*, scenting the air in spring with profuse yellow blooms, Marbleleaf or Putaputaweta *Carpodetus serratus*, Broadleaf *Griselinia littoralis*, Whiteywood or Mahoe *Melicytus ramiflorus* and the world's largest tree fuchsia, Kotukutuku *Fuchsia excorticata*, whose delicious dark-purple drupes ripen in early summer for birds to gorge upon. These species are still common and regenerate well. The Leith Valley, notably Nicols Creek, holds some outstanding specimens of Kotukutuku.

At higher sites and especially inland, the tall forest is more likely to comprise silver beech *Nothofagus menziesii*, often in association with the podocarps Totara and Matai. The Waipori Valley is a silver beech stronghold. Small patches occur on the slopes of Mt Cargill, Flagstaff and Mihiwaka facing Otago Harbour – the closest silver beech to metropolitan Dunedin. There are larger stands on the slopes of Maungatua and the Silver Peaks and at Evansdale, usually with Hall's totara, and a few trees are spread among the podocarps in the Taieri River forest close to sea level near Taieri Mouth.

Fossil pollen studies suggest that 6,000-8,000 years ago, when there was a milder climate with less seasonal difference, Totara and Matai forest was much more extensive on inland sites now occupied by silver beech. A climate change – towards seasonal extremes of cold, wet winters and warm, dry summers – favoured the spread of silver beech. Natural

Below: *Among the more distinctive spiders of the Dunedin forest is the large, colourful and common tunnelweb spider* Porrhothele antipodiana, *which builds thick webs under logs and stones.*

It was the first New Zealand spider to be named. It possesses many primitive features such as up-and-down movements of its fangs and the presence of four book lungs on the underside of its abdomen. This method of breathing means it must seek out dark and moist habitats where prey consists of beetles and other invertebrates.

Despite its somewhat awesome appearance it is not poisonous, but it may bite if squeezed or handled roughly. The male tunnelweb spider wanders about during the mating season and at this time may enter buildings. The best way to deal with them is to coax them gently into a jar and deposit them outside.

R.R. Forster

Left: *Forest characters. Clockwise from bottom left: Peripatus, Hounds tongue fern, Mistletoe on Silver beech, Matai, New Zealand pigeon or Kukupa, South Island robin or Toutouwai, Aoraia moth.*

fires and those caused by early Maori made inroads on the forest to the benefit of the fire-tolerant tussock grasslands.

As in the past, the distribution of forest is influenced by climate, in particular the rainfall pattern. The Mt Cargill-Swampy Summit-Silver Peaks area is rather wetter than the Maungatua Range, due largely to cloudier conditions associated with sea breezes. Vegetation intercepts the moisture in the mists, adding to the precipitation. On Mt Cargill, annual rainfall of 1,000mm is expected in the cloud belt above the 500m contour line (the city centre near sea level has an annual average of about 785mm). Further inland, along the skyline between Flagstaff, Swampy Summit and the Silver Peaks, above 500m, rainfall averages about 1,200mm a year.

The absence or relative rarity in the Dunedin area of several native tree species has long puzzled botanists. Southern rata *Metrosideros umbellata*, so common in the South Otago coastal forest, runs out just south of Taieri Mouth. Kamahi *Weinmannia racemosa*, so common in the south and on the West Coast, also meets a natural boundary at Taieri Mouth. The only naturally-occurring Kamahi in Dunedin are a few specimens in Mill Creek (southern Maungatua) and the Leith Valley, and at Grahams Bush between Sawyers Bay and Mt Cargill.

Compared to northern regions, the Dunedin forest contains only a small number of tall tree species. But the subcanopy and understorey trees, shrubs and lianes are a diverse lot, adding delightful variation in form and colour.

KAPUKATAUMAHAKA Mt Cargill's other name

The highest peak overlooking Otago Harbour is named after William Cargill, co-founder of Otago's Scottish settlement (1848). But Mt Cargill (680m) has another name – Kapukataumahaka. Within this single Maori word is a tale that combines botany, birdlife and bush survival skills.

Kapuka is the name for Broadleaf *Griselinia littoralis*, and taumahaka refers to the snaring of birds at a water-trough. The slopes of Mt Cargill were renowned for their Kapuka trees, which attracted Kukupa, the New Zealand pigeon. When the pigeons ate Kapuka berries they became thirsty, hence the use of water troughs by Maori hunters, who set snares over them.

Broadleaf is abundant today around Dunedin in a subcanopy situation and in open or disturbed areas, reaching a height of about 15m. It is among the hardiest of New Zealand's trees, reaching 900m above sea level and capable of enduring very dry conditions. Its flowers are greenish and so, too, are the immature fruits, which darken when ready to drop.

Below: *The zigzag moth* Charixena iridoxa, *whose white larvae live in the base of the* Astelia *leaves. Although the larvae remain more or less stationary, their feeding produces a zigzag effect on the leaves emerging from the base. Mt Cargill has the only colony of this moth in Dunedin City. It is mainly found in the mountains of the Main Divide.*

Another moth Tmetolophota purdii, *more widespread, feeds on* Astelia. *Its fat green caterpillars create large holes on the leaves (see right). The handsome orange adult was first described from Fairfield.*

Brian Patrick

Right: *Featured on the $100 note, the Zebra moth* Declana egregia *is common in the higher-altitude forests of Dunedin where the cryptic larvae feed on Three-finger foliage. The adults are nocturnal and depend on their resemblance to tree-trunk lichens for camouflage by day.*

Above: *Kotukutuku* tree fuchsia overtops a garden of the bush lily *Astelia fragrans*, Leith Saddle Track. Some leaves of the *Astelia* have been eaten by caterpillars.

LEITH SADDLE Podocarp potpourri

An outstanding podocarp-cedar forest greets travellers at the high point on Dunedin's Northern Motorway – Leith Saddle, 390m above sea level. In addition to the dark-green conical form of New Zealand cedar or Kaikawaka *Libocedrus bidwillii*, the emergent trees are chiefly of the podocarp group – Rimu *Dacrydium cupressinum*, Miro *Prumnopitys ferruginea* (both near their upper limit) and Hall's or Thin-barked totara *Podocarpus hallii*.

Rimu, recognisable by its drooping olive-green foliage, and Totara both produce seed that rests neatly on a small brightly-coloured basal fruit (hence podocarp – 'seed on a foot'); Miro, belonging to a genus that means 'plum fruit', produces drupes that contain the seed. The drupe is large, reddish and irresistible to New Zealand pigeons.

Medium-sized trees of Mahoe, Kotukutuku and Three-finger (Orihou) *Pseudopanax colensoi* overtop shrubs that include the abundant Hupiro *Coprosma foetidissima*, whose crushed leaves smell of dung, hence its unflattering common name Stinkwood. In the New Zealand forest there is nothing quite like Kotukutuku *Fuchsia excorticata* and from the Leith Saddle boardwalk it can be inspected close up. The bark is orange-brown, tissue-thin and always peeling; the flowers are a mixture of green, red and purple and the pollen a vivid blue – colours that speak of this tree's tropical origins.

Notable ground-cover plants are the Crown fern *Blechnum discolor* and the bush lily *Astelia fragrans*. Among the abundant epiphytic filmy ferns hangs the curiously shaped stems of *Tmesipteris tannensis*, the most primitive of vascular plants, with curved pointed leaf-like blades.

LEITH VALLEY Rainforest and Glow Worms

On the city side of the Leith Saddle, the valley features rainforest that has an abundance and diversity of bryophytes to rival Fiordland. Nicols Falls is a 12m-high forest-enclosed waterfall on a tributary of the Leith. It takes 15min to walk to from the Leith Valley Road and at one time was a popular scenic attraction for visitors and Dunedin residents, complemented after dark by a display of glow worms on the ravine walls of Nicols Creek. The glow worm *Arachnocampa luminosa* is the larva of a native fly (a long-legged fungus gnat, seldom seen). To catch food, the 2-4cm-long larvae lower sticky threads and attract prey by emitting a bluish light that can be turned off and on at will. The New Zealand glow worm, which has a 12-month life cycle, is not related to its European namesake, which is a beetle that uses light to attract a mate.

New Zealand pigeon or Kukupa Hemiphaga novaeseelandiae *is one of the most conspicuous birds of the Leith Valley/Woodhaugh/Botanic Gardens area. Kowhai flowers and Miro fruit figure prominently in the diet of these birds, which play a key role in forest ecology as seed dispersers. They are among the world's most beautifully coloured pigeon species. They nest in trees and raise a single chick each breeding season.*

When laden with Miro berries, Kukupa fly sluggishly with a characteristic whistling laboured wingbeat. But they can be surprisingly agile in the air. In what is thought to be territorial displays, they will perform a highly spectacular pattern of stalls and swoops. Pigeons on routine flights occasionally crash into plate-glass windows of houses overlooking Leith Valley.

Left: *October blossoms in the Leith Valley/Pinehill area – Lemonwood or Tarata* Pittosporum eugenioides *flowers prolifically in spring. Its common name derives from the lemon scent exuded by the leaves when crushed. Lemonwood resin was used by Maori as chewing gum.*

Right: *Silvereye feeding on nectar of Kowhai* Sophora microphylla *in full flower on the cliffs above Woodhaugh Gardens. The flowers attract numerous birds, including Tui, Bellbird, and New Zealand pigeon. At least five moth species specialise in feeding on various parts of the Kowhai.*

WOODHAUGH Relict Swamp Forest

Within Woodhaugh Gardens on the banks of the Water of Leith lies a small remnant of Kahikatea swamp forest – the only example left in Dunedin district. Kahikatea or White pine *Dacrycarpus dacrydioides* was once abundant in fertile low-lying areas, typically on alluvial soils. New Zealand's tallest native tree, reaching 60m, it was plundered last century for its soft, pale and odourless timber, valuable for old-style butterboxes. A few specimens are prominent with Matai in pasture on the river flats near Waitati, close to State Highway 1, and there are a number of large Kahikatea trees on the banks of the Taieri River upstream from the Taieri Mouth bridge and at Woodside on the Taieri Plain.

At Woodhaugh the Kahikatea is associated with Matai or Black Pine, Lacebark and Lowland ribbonwood. Some of the native trees in the vicinity have been planted, notably Red beech *Nothofagus fusca*.

The elegant moth Hydriomena arida *was first described from Dunedin and thought to be locally extinct until it was rediscovered in damp gullies in the Leith Valley. A nocturnal moth, it is shown here on shield fern. The larvae feed on* Gunnera monoica *on damp banks.*

Prominent subcanopy trees are Tarata *Pittosporum eugenioides*, Mahoe *Melicytus ramiflorus* and Milk tree or Turepo *Streblus heterophyllus*, whose common name refers to the milky sap that exudes from the stems in spring. Less common at Woodhaugh and the Dunedin area generally is a shrubby small-leaved relative of Mahoe, *Melicytus micranthus*. Found perching on a variety of shrubs and trees is the broad-leaved mistletoe *Ileostylus micranthus*, which has tiny yellow flowers and yellow berries.

Streblus moths

The exquisitely coloured moth *Phycomorpha metachrysa* is the smaller of two uncommon moths whose larvae are found feeding on Milk tree *Streblus heterophyllus* in Woodhaugh Gardens. The larger of the two is *Meterana octans*, whose fat bright-green larvae are well camouflaged in the foliage of Milk tree. The former was first described from the Dunedin area, and its larvae feed within the diseased spikes of the plant.

Left: *Southern rata flowering in the Town Belt. Rata does not grow naturally in the city.*

TOWN BELT

A 4.5km-long green belt dissects the hill suburbs of metropolitan Dunedin between the Southern Cemetery and the Botanic Gardens, providing the city with a conspicuous array of native and introduced trees dating from last century. Following the clearance of much of the area, native and introduced species were planted in many areas and regeneration filled out the protected corridor, known as the Town Belt. More than 200 tree and shrub species are found here.

At the northern end, the light-demanding Kanuka *Kunzea ericoides* is a feature tree, occupying drier sites. Its presence indicates total clearance of the original forest cover. Some Kanuka – 30cm in diameter and 15m tall – are overmature and beginning to collapse. Associated with Kanuka are Broadleaf *Griselinia littoralis*, Mapou *Myrsine australis*, and Pate *Schefflera digitata*. Another prominent tree is Kotukutuku *Fuchsia excorticata*, which relishes the shady faces found across much of the Town Belt.

Remnant tall podocarps are dotted throughout and there are a few young self-sown Rimu, Totara and Matai

Forest moth

Dunedin is the only New Zealand city with a resident species of Aoraia, a large Hepialid moth. Adult males of *Aoraia rufivena* (pictured), which have a wingspan of about 7cm, are often attracted to city lights. The winged but flightless female scatters eggs about the forest floor. The species also occurs in snowgrass communities. It has an annual lifecycle, with adults emerging between late January and May. Despite its size and conspicuousness, this moth was named only recently, in 1994. It is related to the native Porina moth, a pest of exotic pasture.

establishing. Lacebark *Hoheria populnea* and its narrow-leaved cousin, *H. angustifolia* are represented, as is Lowland ribbonwood or Manatu, *Plagianthus regius*, a tree reaching 17m with form and foliage vastly different from Saltmarsh ribbonwood. There are large planted specimens of Red beech *Nothofagus fusca* and Southern rata *Metrosideros umbellata*. Several shrubs outside their natural limits also thrive in the Town Belt, notably Rangiora *Brachyglottis repanda* and Raurekau *Coprosma grandiflora*. Rangiora, which bears unmistakably large oblong leaves, white underneath, forms hedges if trimmed, as on the road to Purakaunui above Port Chalmers. Its natural southern limit is Kaikoura.

Throughout the Town Belt, and colouring it in autumn, are magnificent examples of exotic deciduous trees, now fully mature, including European beech, English oak, Sycamore and Elm. Towards the southern end especially, they create a woodland effect.

The leaf litter fauna, as in forest environments throughout New Zealand, is rich in spiders, insects and micro-snails. One tiny snail from the Town Belt, *Alsolemia cresswelli*, is a Dunedin endemic species. A recent survey recorded 46 micro-snail species in the metropolitan area.

> **Problem plant**
>
> Old Man's Beard *Clematis vitalba*, a noxious deciduous climber, delights in establishing in areas such as the Town Belt. Without control, it will invade and eventually overwhelm native vegetation.
>
> It was introduced into New Zealand last century as an ornamental plant but has since spread to become a threat in many areas. It is well-known for its grey tufted seed balls that are conspicuous in autumn and persist through winter after the leaves are lost. Older stems are grey and ribbed; younger stems are purple and downy.
>
> Old Man's Beard is difficult to control. It must be dug out by the roots to be destroyed. Broken bits left lying around will readily resprout. The cut roots or stumps can be poisoned and the foliage burnt.

Neville Peat

Right: *Marbleleaf or Putaputaweta* Carpodetus serratus *produces abundant flowers in December-January. An attractive New Zealand endemic, it grows to about 10m. It is host to a parasitic shrub, a kind of mistletoe* Tupeia antarctica, *whose white, purple-flecked berries were a food of the Maori.*

CAVERSHAM Peripatus

In the leaf litter of Caversham Valley's moist bushed gullies, which form the southern limit of the Town Belt, lives a small velvety caterpillar-like creature (see photo, below) that is of exceptional interest to science. Growing to over 3cm in length, it belongs to an ancient group of invertebrates called Peripatus – believed to be the missing link between worms (*Annelida*) and the centipedes, insects, spiders and crustaceans (*Arthropoda*).

Although resembling a caterpillar or centipede, the Peripatus does not have a head marked off from the rest of the body nor any external sign of segmentation. Only about 100 species of Peripatus are known to science, although it is a group spread across South-east Asia, Africa, South America, Australia and New Zealand. While some species lay eggs, others give birth to live young and some even have a placenta through which nutrients are delivered to developing embryos.

Young of the Caversham Peripatus are born alive and family groups stay together for some time. The Caversham animal is a voracious carnivore. To entrap its prey it shoots out streams of sticky fluid from turrets on either side of its head. Despite urban development and clearance of much of its habitat, this Peripatus has survived. The Caversham species, together with a new species from the Leith Valley, are of international significance. New Zealand has only five described species in a world tally of fewer than 100. In 1993, the Dunedin City Council with the assistance of the Royal Forest and Bird Protection Society purchased a 4ha area of Caversham Bush to extend and protect the habitat of this extraordinary animal.

Below: *New Zealand Long-tailed bat* Chalinolobus tuberculatus, *one of the world's micro-bats, has been reported from the Silver Stream forest. The nearest populations are in the Catlins.*

Rod Morris

Brian Patrick

Left: *The Caversham Peripatus.*

SILVER STREAM Refuge for Robins

A small isolated population of South Island robin or Toutouwai *Petroica australis* inhabits native and planted forests in the Silver Stream catchment in the vicinity of Whare Flat. As the only robins in east Otago, the population is of major interest to ornithologists and conservationists. Robins require forested areas to disperse and are unlikely ever to have contact with the nearest populations – on the Blue Mountains and at Waikaia Bush in northern Southland, 115km westward. The Silver Stream robins' habitat includes Kanuka, Manuka and regenerating native broadleaved forest, but the birds are also found in old plantations of exotic trees, part of the Flagstaff block. Commonly found on or close to the forest floor (hence their vulnerability to stoats, wild cats and other predators), they eat insects and other invertebrates and will draw near to people strolling in their territories in the hope the intruders will stir or scuff up new food. The rotational logging of plantation trees for timber and clear-felling of Kanuka and Manuka for firewood may pose difficulties for the robins in the future.

Below: *Silver beech forest flanking Waipori River.*

Neville Peat

WAIPORI Silver beech stronghold

Waipori Valley, south of Maungatua, contains the largest remnant silver beech forest in eastern South Island north of the Catlins region. Silver beech is spread throughout Waipori Falls Scenic Reserve (1322ha), Dunedin's largest scenic reserve, which occupies the central portion of the valley. Across about a quarter of the reserve it forms a pure forest; elsewhere it is emergent with Podocarp trees, mainly Rimu, Matai, and Totara or gives way to kanuka/manuka woodland. From the mouth of the gorge it expands across the southern face of Maungatua and is clearly visible from the Taieri Plain.

Silver beech or Tawhai is the most widely distributed of New Zealand's five kinds of beech (Red, Hard, Silver, Mountain and Black). It forms the treeline through much of the wetter regions of western Otago and Fiordland. None of the other beech species – the larger-leaved Red and Hard beech and the smaller-leaved, smooth-edged Mountain and Black beech – is found naturally in the Dunedin area, although there are planted examples of them all, especially Red beech.

Rod Morris

Left: *A pair of South Island Rifleman* Acanthisitta chloris chloris *at their nest, with food for chicks. The Rifleman is New Zealand's smallest native bird. Another small forest bird, restricted to South Island forests, is Brown creeper or Pipipi* Mohoua novaeseelandiae. *It is common in Waipori forest. In the non-breeding season flocks of Brown creeper trickle through the canopy, keeping contact with a repetitive trilling call and often in the company of numbers of Silvereye, Grey warbler and South Island fantail. Brown creeper is a host for Long-tailed cuckoo.*

Right: *Prickly shield fern Polystichum vestitum, Waipori Valley.*

The Waipori forest is bordered in the south by an extensive planted forest of *Pinus radiata* and in the north by shrubland and tussock grassland on the shoulder of the Maungatua Range. The native forest is a mosaic of types. A visitor can sample beech, podocarp, kanuka and a range of broad-leaved trees on the walking tracks in the vicinity of the picnic ground in the lower valley. The same area hosts an array of birdlife, including Bellbird, Grey warbler, Silvereye, Brown creeper, South Island fantail, New Zealand pigeon and Shining cuckoo.

The silver beech trees are host to red mistletoe *Peraxilla colensoi*, which produces abundant scarlet flowers in December-January. There is a good place to see mistletoe halfway up the valley at a clearing on the banks of the Waipori River. Another accessible red mistletoe habitat is close to the picnic ground at Woodside, upstream of which large silver beech trees are garlanded with flowers of the parasite at the festive season.

The Waipori forest is home to a rich assortment of insects, among them the only Dunedin records of the moths *Austrocidaria parora* and *Asaphodes obarata*, the latter nationally rare.

Eastern rosella

Larger and much more brightly coloured than native parakeets, Eastern rosellas have established wild populations on the outskirts of the Dunedin metropolitan area since their introduction from Australia in about 1910. Singly or in flocks they are reasonably common in the upper Leith Valley (especially around Sullivans Dam), Waitati/Orokonui, Woodside (west Taieri) and Waipori Valley. They favour forest margins and lightly wooded areas, and nest in spring, mainly in holes in trees. Their call when alarmed is a loud parrot-like screech.

Chapter 7   UPLANDS High country potpourri

Beyond the coastal hills and the angular volcanic peaks overlooking Otago Harbour is a largely treeless upland environment of exposed ridges and plateaux, snow tussock communities, shrubby gullies and wetlands. Not as high as the ranges on the city perimeter (Maungatua, Lammermoor and Rock and Pillar) but skyline-makers nonetheless, the uplands include landscape features such as the Silver Peaks (777m), Swampy Summit (739m) and neighbouring Flagstaff (668m), Swampy Hill (733m) on the northern boundary of the city near Nenthorn, Mt Watkin (616m) inland from Waikouaiti, and Taieri Ridge (708m).

The Swampy-Flagstaff complex separates the Leith and Silver Stream catchments; the Silver Peaks main ridge divides the Waikouaiti and Taieri catchments; Mt Watkin holds the high ground to the north of the Waikouaiti River's north branch; and Taieri Ridge separates the Strath Taieri from the Moonlight/Macraes district.

Except for Flagstaff, which lies on a popular walking track overlooking the city centre, these upland features are little visited but well worth exploring for their distinctive array of plants and fauna. Among the most surprising aspects is the presence of extensive and species-rich wetlands, a habitat more commonly associated with valley floors.

Before the Mt Cargill road was built (superseded this century by the Northern Motorway), the main route north to Waikouaiti lay across the open country and moderate grades of Flagstaff and Swampy Summit, which were called the 'Snowy Mountains' for a time. Known to Maori as Whakari (after which the adjacent suburb of Wakari is named) Flagstaff is like a 'forehead' on the city landscape, high and prominent. It acquired its European name from the nineteenth century practice of hoisting a flag at its high point to let European settlers on the Taieri know of the arrival of an immigrant vessel at Port Chalmers or Dunedin.

Flagstaff and Swampy Summit are volcanic creations, as is the solitary round knob of Mt Watkin. The Silver Peaks and Taieri Ridge are built of schist, although there are volcanic protuberances on Taieri Ridge in the form of The Sisters and The Crater.

The land tenure of the uplands is mixed. The designations include scenic reserve (Department of Conservation and Dunedin City Council), water and timber reserve (DCC), pastoral leasehold and freehold. About 2,500ha of land in the Silver Peaks area formerly managed by the Dunedin City Council as water and timber reserve is to be included in the Silver Peaks Scenic Reserve, which will make the reserve one of Otago's largest at over 3,500ha.

Kaikawaka

The pyramidal or cone form of New Zealand cedar or Kaikawaka *Libocedrus bidwillii*, stands out in the cloud forest of Leith Saddle. It also cuts a striking profile in high forest in the Silver Peaks area and on the flanks of Mt Cargill, Flagstaff and Swampy Summit.

After about 15 minutes climb up the Leith Saddle Track, one is rewarded by a close encounter with a rich native cedar forest. Kaikawaka grows to a height of about 15m on this ridge. The trunk is tapered, the bark light brown and decidedly stringy. Lower branches are bulky and often jut at right angles to the trunk, making the tree's distinctive form.

Old spars, silvery with age and clearly hard-wearing, are prominently scattered about the canopy. The death of so many cedars while still standing may be due to climate change.

Left: *Uplands symbols. Clockwise from bottom left: Lycopodium club moss,* Blechnum capense *or Kiokio fern, Three-finger shrub or Orihou, Tussock butterfly* Argyrophenga janitae, *New Zealand cedar or Kaikawaka, South Island Tomtit or Ngiru-ngiru, Peppertree or Horopito.*

Left: *A feature of upland areas is the Australasian harrier* Circus approximans, *pictured here feeding on a dead hare. A large bird of prey, it is typically seen gliding across open areas with its long wings forming a shallow V. Harriers nest around swamps over summer, following a courtship that usually involves spectacular diving, soaring and tumbling flights. About the only time their calls are heard is at courtship – a high-pitched plaintive see-oo.*

Since European settlement, harriers have increased in number and extended their range due to the clearance of forest and the introduction of small mammals, notably rabbits, which have served to increase their food supply. Although they will take live prey, they readily scavenge road kills and are themselves often run down by vehicles.

The harrier, self-introduced from Australia, is about a third larger than the endemic New Zealand falcon (see page 103), our only other surviving day-time bird of prey. Maori know the harrier as Kahu.

Orchids

Sun orchids of the genus *Thelymitra* are eye-catching on Swampy Summit and Flagstaff in late summer and early autumn. Sometimes found singly, sometimes in groups, the sun orchids present their flowers on tall stalks. Two species (*T. venosa* and *T. hatchii*) have blue flowers; the more common *T. longifolia* has white ones with purple and yellow centres. Other ground orchids common in upland grasslands or near bush or forest are the white orchid *Caladenia lyallii*; the horizontal or beak orchid *Lyperanthus antarcticus*, which holds its yellow-green flowers (usually two) curiously horizontal; the odd-leaved orchid *Aporostylis bifolia*, which has two unequally-sized hairy leaves and white flowers with yellow dots on the lip; and the onion orchid *Microtis unifolia*, which has only one leaf and arranges its myriad tiny yellow-green flowers on a tall spike.

Bottom left: *The horizontal orchid* Lyperanthus antarcticus *on a moss bed, Swampy Summit.*

Right: Celmisia hookeri, *an uncommon daisy, is found on the sweeping upland plateau of Swampy Hill 25km north-west of Waikouaiti near Dunedin's northern boundary. Its large, soft leaves form rosettes up to about 50cm wide. Its last refuges are in north-east Otago, including the Horse Range, and, somewhat surprisingly, northern Southland (Nokomai Gorge; Slate Range). The daisy has suffered from grazing, fires and unscrupulous collecting for garden use. A rare grass* Simplicia laxa *was recently rediscovered at Nenthorn near Swampy Hill.*

Above: *Copper tussock* Chionochloa rubra cuprea *on Swampy Summit. In the distance is Flagstaff.*

Snow tussock communities

Tall snow tussocks give the uplands a distinctive tawny colour and soft texture. Where undisturbed, they develop impressive size and density, and will grow to over 2m in height – a low 'forest', long-lived.

The most important tussock species in the Dunedin uplands – and across the Otago rangelands – is Narrow-leaved snow tussock *Chionochloa rigida*. Its flowerheads overtop the leaves, a habit which distinguishes it from Red tussock *C. rubra*, whose flowerheads are generally held within the foliage. Red tussock's southern subspecies, *C. rubra cuprea*, known also as Copper tussock on account of the colour of its leaves, mixes with Narrow-leaved snow tussock on Swampy Summit. A larger but less abundant species, *C. conspicua*, more commonly associated with shrubland and forest margins, has broader leaves and conspicuous flowerheads that are similar to but more branched than Toetoe *Cortaderia richardii*.

Over the last thousand years, fires lit by early Maori allowed tussock grassland to spread into areas once dominated by forest or shrubland.

Tussock is a word derived from the Old English term, 'tusk', meaning a tuft of hair. And indeed tall tussocks are hair-like on the landscape, waving and rippling in the wind.

SWAMPY SUMMIT/FLAGSTAFF

'A wonderful gift of Nature to Dunedin'
– A.H. Reed (publisher/writer),
describing Flagstaff, 1954

For anyone interested in botany and insects, the adjoining tops of Swampy Summit and Flagstaff represent a fascinating subalpine experience within sight and easy striking distance of the city centre.

One of the most distinctive plants is the speargrass or Wild Spaniard. Swampy Summit is a key habitat for *Aciphylla scott-thomsonii*, the tallest and stoutest of New Zealand's 40-odd species of speargrass (type locality, Maungatua Range). Its massive clumps of stiff glaucous (blue-green) leaves can reach over 1m in height, out of which rise flowerheads up to 3m tall. Although common on Swampy Summit, it is scarce on neighbouring Flagstaff, where the smaller Golden speargrass *A. aurea* prevails. The latter, common throughout the Otago uplands, has leaves edged yellow. The whole plant has a golden hue. *A. glaucescens* is smaller, with narrow bluish-green leaves. The slender-leaved *A. subflabellata* is found on the north-west slopes of Swampy Summit, towards the Silver Peaks area. Its southern limit is Black Head but it may be extinct there. A small colony survives among flax on the cliffs south of St Clair.

Above: *Clumps of the giant speargrass* Aciphylla scott-thomsonii, *bearing flowerheads over 2m tall, on the northern slopes of Swampy Summit, facing the Silver Stream catchment and the Silver Peaks.*

Right: *Tauhinu or Cottonwood* Cassinia vauvilliersii, *in flower, growing over a bed of the colourful fern Kiokio* Blechnum capense *on Swampy Summit.*

The genus *Aciphylla* is found only in New Zealand and Australia, with Australia having just two species. Botanists have long puzzled over why they evolved such sharp armoury in a land that lacked browsing mammals. One theory held that the spines and needle-tipped leaves constituted a defence against trampling and browsing by moa. But there is also speculation that the spines are not a defence at all but an evolutionary response to chronic drought in the distant past. The stiff spiny foliage enables the plant to create room for itself among the snow tussocks and shrubs.

Across the Swampy Summit/Flagstaff tops the vegetation is dominated by snow tussock and mountain flax *Phormium cookianum.* Post-European fires induced a comprehensive cover of snow tussock but the shrubs are reinvading in many areas. Manuka *Leptospermum scoparium,* Inaka or Grass tree *Dracophyllum longifolium* and Tauhinu or Cottonwood *Cassinia vauvilliersii* are migrating upwards from strongholds near the forest edge. Other shrubs making inroads on the tussock grasslands are *Hebe (Leonohebe) odora*, notable for its neatly rounded bushes and clusters of white flowers at the branch tips, Three-finger *Pseudopanax colensoi*, which produces flowers (white) and fruit (purple black) on large umbels, and the tree daisy *Olearia aborescens*. Manuka is expected to predominate in the medium-term, with the likelihood it will eventually be succeeded by native forest (New Zealand cedar/broadleaf), if fire can be excluded. Grasslands are expected to persist longer on the cooler tops, however. The shrubland/forest succession has prompted a suggestion that the lower slopes of the Flagstaff area be burnt every 15-20 years, in spring, in order to retain the snow tussock cover for which the scenic reserve was created, as well as for its educational, ecological and recreational values.

There is a threat of wilding tree infestation from the large plantation of exotic trees (mainly *Pinus radiata*, Douglas fir and European larch) growing on the south-western slopes of Flagstaff and Swampy Summit.

Wetter conditions on the top of Swampy Summit, where there are peat layers and extensive bogs, could inhibit the development of woody species much beyond what is already established – low-growing shrubs such as *Coprosma cheesemanii, C. ciliata* and *C. rugosa*, the Daphne relative *Pimelea oreophila*, and an occasional Turpentine shrub *Dracophyllum uniflorum*, which is a bronze-leaved, more prostrate relative of the Grass tree. Among the Coprosma species, *C. rugosa* stands out because of its reddish-brown bark.

Dwarf shrubs filling gaps between tussocks and flax, and often only ankle-high, include *Pentachrondra pumila*, which is distinguished by its relatively large scarlet berries (up to 12mm diameter and hollow), *Cyathodes empetrifolia*, and Snowberries *Gaultheria depressa* and *G. (Pernettya) macrostigma*.

> Swampy Summit has two species of the poisonous shrub Tutu – the broad-leaved *Coriaria sarmentosa* and feather-leaved *C. plumosa*.

Flowers and fruit: An undescribed narrow-leaved Celmisia *daisy (left), common on damper sites on Swampy Summit, and (right) the showy fruit of* Pentachondra pumila *surrounded by* Gaultheria (Pernettya) macrostigma *and* Cyathodes empetrifolia, *bottom left.*

The Painted Forest

The 75ha Painted Forest is the largest patch of Silver beech left in the Silver Peaks, a pure stand reaching an altitude of 700m, west of the tallest peak – Silver Peak No. 2 (777m). A dark-green island in a tawny sea of tussock, it provides graphic evidence of the way vegetation can change with a shift in rock types. It is located on schist soils close to the boundary with volcanic landforms, where podocarp and broadleaved trees predominate. The Painted Forest and other Silver beech remnants in the Silver Peaks are spreading very slowly, with seedlings softening the margin of the mature trees. The Silver Peaks marks a climatic boundary, too, with the land to the west becoming drier and less influenced by coastal conditions.

All are members of the Heath family and all produce berries, red, white or pink. The two Snowberries, once in separate genera, have been grouped in the same genus because they hybridise.

The commonest member of the lily family on Swampy Summit and Flagstaff is *Astelia nervosa*, whose stiffly arching, silver-tinged leaves form clumps up to 1m across. Its orange berries are inconspicuous compared to the bold fruiting of its relative, the bush lily *Astelia fragrans*. Among the mountain daisies, the commonest is a narrow-leaved species resembling *Celmisia gracilenta*, which has delicately petalled white flowers that may be found dotted about in open spaces. It is often seen in the company of the Maori onion *Bulbinella angustifolia*, whose yellow flowerheads are prominent in early summer, and the native Harebell *Wahlenbergia albomarginata*, which can have white or pale blue flowers.

Damper places, including moist banks, allow the ubiqitous fern Kiokio *Blechnum capense* to display its attractive reddish foliage. Also present is the rhizomatous *Gunnera monoica*.

Around the Swampy Summit bogs prominent plant species include the cushions of Comb sedge *Oreobolus strictus* and the native Anemone, *Anemone tenuicaulis*, with *Kelleria laxa* occupying slightly drier sites. Strangely, the more widespread *K. dieffenbachii* is absent here but it is common on other low-alpine areas and areas of exposed peat with wood remains of Pink pine and occasional rounded quartz pebbles – actually moa gizzard stones.

Insect heritage

The Dunedin uplands have inherited a rich and colourful array of insects, some of which are possibly descended from species that inhabited the alpine zone of the cooled volcano, following the cessation of volcanic activity about 10 million years ago.

Underlining the long ancestry of the invertebrate communities is the presence of species with flightless females or with both sexes flightless, rendering them relatively immobile. Many species are active by day.

The key groups are grasshoppers, bugs, beetles, flies, wasps, caddis and moths.

Three butterfly species breed above the treeline in the upland and subalpine zones – the Common Copper *Lycaena salustius* on Muehlenbeckia and two Tussock butterflies *Argyrophenga antipodum* and *A. janitae*. The latter is less common and faster through the air. The Tussock butterflies may be seen flying together over snowgrass, the larval food plant.

Ground beetles (Carabidae) are another outstanding element of the fauna. Many tribes of this large family are represented in the uplands. Notable among the species is *Oregus inaequalis*, whose only known modern locality is Swampy Summit. Longhorn beetles use the widespread shrub *Hebe odora* as a larval home. Adults are common on the Hebe stems in summer. Another insect that uses this shrub as a food plant is the tiny and rarely-seen diurnal moth *Scythris nigra*, whose equally tiny larvae do a lot of damage.

Two species of Cicada of the genus *Kikihia*, inhabit the uplands. *Kikihia angusta*, whose males are pale yellow-brown and females pale green, is common on the grasslands. A brighter green species, undescribed, is associated with shrublands.

Above: *The carabid* Oregus inaequalis *on moss, Swampy Summit.*

The rare diurnal moth Scoparia tuicana *was described from the 'Waitati Hills' in 1926. It has been rediscovered on Swampy Summit. Its only other known locations are Maungatua and Slopedown Range in the Catlins. It is at home in wetlands or damp snowgrass areas.*

Left: *This newly-discovered stonefly species of the genus* Apteryoperla *lives in copper tussock. Both adults and larvae use the moist habitat deep within the tussock. A wingless species, it is known only from Swampy Summit and the Blue Mountains. By contrast, most other stonefly species are associated with flowing fresh water.*

Above: *Longhorn beetle* Mesolamia marmorata *was described from the Dunedin area, where it is locally common on* Hebe (Leonohebe) odora *shrubs.*

Above: *One of the most ancient moths is* Sabatinca quadrijuga, *whose tiny day-flying adults appear on damp sites in September-October. They are common on Mt Cargill. The adults possess jaws instead of a sucking tube. Larvae feed on another ancient plant group – liverworts.*

Below: *Diurnal geometrid moths like* Dasyuris transaurea *are a feature of insect communities in the Dunedin uplands. Its striking patterning and bold colours are butterfly-like. The 100 or so similar species make up for a lack of butterflies in our fauna. The caterpillars of this species feed on* Anisotome aromatica, *with the adults emerging in November.*

Right: *Two representatives of the order* Orthoptera *(includes crickets, grasshoppers and weta): a common short-horned grasshopper* Sigaus australis *(top) and an undescribed cave weta (bottom) that lives in tunnels in Sphagnum moss.*

Right: *The insect-eating New Zealand Pipit (Pihoihoi)* Anthus novaeseelandiae *is commonly seen in tussock grassland areas, attracting attention by the way it flicks its tail. It runs with a dipping motion and flies swiftly. Because of its mottled brown colouring, the Pipit is often confused with another bird of the uplands, the Skylark, introduced from Britain last century. The Pipit is more slender, with a longer, finer bill and no crest. It does not hover like the Skylark, whose warbling flight song is distinctive, and it is less likely to be seen over pasture. Both birds nest on the ground, concealing their nests. A Pipit's nest is especially hard to find.*

MT WATKIN/HIKAROROA

Mt Watkin (Hikaroroa), 8km west of Waikouaiti and 616m above sea level, is an oddity – a volcanic hill standing alone amidst a schist landscape, advertising its volcanic origins with an impressive series of radiating basalt boulder screes. Not only is the landform special; the slopes of Mt Watkin contain some rare and peculiar plants.

Speargrasses abound, protected from grazing by the water reserve status of Mt Watkin. The slender-leaved and palatable speargrass *Aciphylla subflabellata* occurs here along with the larger bluish-green *A. glaucescens* and golden *A. aurea*. Also present is *Fuchsia perscandens*, a scrambling relative of the high-profile tree fuchsia *F. excorticata*. The scrambling species has smaller, rounder and well-spaced leaves and smaller (10mm) flowers from which deep-purple berries form.

Another uncommon plant, clinging to the rock bluffs of Mt Watkin, is a variety of the native aniseed *Gingidia montana*, now

Above: *View south from the Mt Watkin summit, across rock scree and towards part of Garden Bush reserve.*

Below: *The pretty diurnal moth* Cephalissa siria *is found where its host plant* Fuchsia perscandens *survives, notably on Mt Watkin and other hills surrounding Dunedin. A coastal population of this moth occurs at Akatore Creek, south of Taieri Mouth.*

Right: *Two forms of* Gingidia montana *in flower. The form with blue-green leaves is found on the rocky slopes of Mt Watkin and the larger green-leaved form (near right) has now only one population left in the Dunedin region, on the steep upper slopes of Mopanui. The green-leaved form is still plentiful in wetter mountains of the Main Divide.*

Above: *Broadleaf* Griselinia littoralis *forest establishing on one of the rock glaciers on Mt Watkin.*

rare where grazing animals have access to it. The eastern Otago variety is a compact plant with blue-green foliage.

New Zealand's only deciduous Coprosma, *C. virescens* occurs on Mt Watkin. It has distinctive orange-fawn bark on its branches and a trunk that often bears smooth knobbles. The leaves are pale green (as its species name suggests), thin and trowel-shaped. Dunedin is the type locality for this shrub, which is found from Gisborne southwards, especially east of the South Island's Main Divide.

On the more stable 'rock glaciers', patches of low forest have established, with Broadleaf *Griselinia littoralis* and Kohuhu *Pittosporum tenuifolium* forming the bulk of the canopy. Beneath, moss and Hounds tongue fern cover the boulders. Remnant logs of totara testify to the forest cover in pre-human times.

Quarrying of the basalt boulders at the toe of the rock glaciers on the eastern slopes of Mt Watkin presents a threat to the integrity of the landscape.

SUTTON LAKE Worth its salt

New Zealand's only inland salt lake worthy of the name is located at the south end of the Strath Taieri Valley amidst the spectacular tor ridges of Sutton.

Protected since 1991 within a 140ha scenic reserve, Sutton Salt Lake occupies an enclosed shallow basin in the schist landscape, 250m above sea level. Its water is about half as salty as seawater. The salts emanate from the schist rocks, arriving at the lake with surface run-off or by percolating up through the soil. The lake sediments are extremely alkaline.

Reaching a depth of only about 30cm, the lake evaporates in dry spells to become a cracked bed of silt. Salt-tolerant plants line the shore, notably the creeping herbs *Lilaeopsis novae-zelandiae* (type locality, Tomahawk), *Chenopodium ambiguum*, native celery *Apium prostratum* and *Selliera microphylla*, the first three of which are common at the sea coast. Their presence 45km inland has had scientists speculating as to how they got here – whether they might represent an ancient marine shore (the sea could have been this far inland during the Miocene some 25 million years ago) or whether they were brought by sea birds such as Black-backed gulls which are not uncommon here.

No fish live in the lake, but there are tiny salt-adapted aquatic animals, including copepods, rotifers and water beetles – an attraction for ducks and wading birds, including New Zealand shoveler, Mallard, Paradise shelduck, Pied stilt, South Island Pied oystercatcher, Black swan and White-faced heron. Australasian harrier and Spur-winged plover are also common. New Zealand falcons pass this way occasionally.

In the grasslands and shrublands surrounding the lake, native species are benefitting from the absence of stock. Among the five prominent native grasses occurring here (Blue wheatgrass, Silver tussock, Narrow-leaved snow tussock, Blue tussock and Hard tussock), the wheatgrass *Elymus tenuis* is especially significant. Palatable to stock and usu-

Aciphylla subflabellata *is making a comeback in the protected grasslands of Sutton Salt Lake Scenic Reserve.*

Left: *An undescribed native forget-me-not (*Myosotis *species) is found on tor ledges amongst lichens at Sutton Salt Lake Scenic Reserve. Its only other known locations are the Lammermoor Range and the Nenthorn/Macraes area.*

Right: *Sutton Salt Lake, part-filled. In the foreground on cracked mud by the shore are mats of the salt-tolerant* Chenopodium ambiguum.

Neville Peat

> **Lichens**
>
> There are some 1,300 known kinds of lichen in New Zealand, several hundred of which are represented in the Dunedin region. Among the more distinctive Dunedin species are:
>
> *Steinera sorediata*: pale blue-grey, fan-shaped, found on rocks near the summit of Mt Cargill, from where it was described in 1963. A disjunct population occurs on Mt Taranaki.
>
> *Knightiella splachnirima*: pale green, rounded, found on subalpine exposures of peat on Swampy Summit, Silver Peaks and Maungatua. The species also occurs at Seaward Moss near Invercargill and Stewart Island.
>
> Often the first plants to colonise bare ground, lichens are extraordinarily hardy and adaptable. They are found anywhere between sea level and the highest mountains.
>
> Their biology is complex. The fungal component depends on the algal one for energy from photosynthesis and in turn provides the algae with a cosy environment. Thus lichens are ecosystems in themselves, rather than single organisms. Some lichens fix nitrogen in forest and grassland settings.

ally only found on the 'long acre', it is now flourishing in Sutton Salt Lake Scenic Reserve, decorating the grasslands with golden seedheads on long, drooping stems. Also increasing is the speargrass *Aciphylla subflabellata*, rare in the region because of grazing. Shrubs of Corokia, Olearia, Coprosma and Matagouri form the core of the shrublands.

The moths and butterflies include the southern tiger moth, whose presence indicates relatively intact natural values. By late summer the dry grassland reverberates with the crackle of the small native black cricket *Pteronemobius bigelowi* and the larger short-winged katydid *Conocephalus bilineatus*.

Tor ridges in the vicinity, strikingly parallel when viewed from the air, have been exhumed by erosion. The rocks have weathered under the ground as well as at the surface, and the process continues. Only the most resistant elements of the rock remain.

Large skinks at risk

In the rocky uplands of the Strath Taieri, Nenthorn and Macraes Flat areas live populations of two of New Zealand's rarest, largest and most attractive skinks – the Otago skink *Leiolopisma otagense* and the closely related Grand skink *Leiolopisma grande*.

Both have glossy metallic black skin with gold markings. Both bask on schist outcrops on sunny days, waiting to catching passing flies, moths and other invertebrates. They lunge for and grab prey in their mouths. Crevices in the rocks provide hiding places and frost-free homes for the skinks. Their diet is thought to include a range of fruit from Coprosma bushes and the Porcupine shrub *Melicytus alpinus* (formerly

Above and right: *Upland habitats. Tussock grassland (above) on Hummock (736m) in the Nenthorn area near the city's northern boundary; and a typical shrubland gully – in this case, Sutton Stream – dominated by* Coprosma propinqua *and* Muehlenbeckia complexa.

96 Wild Dunedin

Hymenanthera alpina). Lizards may well play a seed-dispersing role for the Porcupine shrub, which secretes its white berries among spiny branches, making them unavailable to birds.

The Otago skink is the larger of the two species, reaching 30cm in length, including tail, and 66.5g in weight. They give birth to two or three live young in early autumn. In warmer countries, lizards usually lay eggs. Live birth is probably a response to a cold climate.

The skinks are known to move between rock outcrops. One marked Otago skink moved 70m in two weeks, and a grand skink was observed to move 139m. Movement over pasture rather than through tussocks grassland may make them more vulnerable to predators. Australasian harrier and New Zealand falcon are natural predators; the wild cat is probably the most dangerous introduced predator, although magpies, ferrets, stoats and rats are also likely to prey on them.

Last century Otago and Grand skinks were found across Otago, having been reported from Rough Ridge, Roxburgh and Queenstown. Now their distribution is limited and scattered, and their future uncertain without pro-active attempts to conserve them. Their two remaining strongholds are the Strath Taieri/Macraes uplands and the Lindis Pass/Hawea district; the Otago skink's plight is serious, with as few as 1,400 left.

Otago skinks (far left) and a Grand skink sunbathing and waiting for prey. The Grand skink is surrounded by lichen of the Xanthoparmelia *species.*

Chris Gaskin

Chapter 8   THE TAIERI   Where falcons fly

Rivers constitute the lifeblood of many cities. Unquestionably, the Taieri River is the Dunedin area's main artery. Together with its many tributaries, the river is at once a water supply (for homes and farms), a playground (angling, boating, swimming), a tourist attraction (Taieri Gorge) and a landscape feature whose moods vary from raw and boisterous to utterly placid. Then there are its intrinsic values – attendant plant and animal life, some of it unique, with ancestry older than the river, older even than the hills and ranges that influence its course.

By the time it reaches Kokonga, the city's north-west boundary, for the run south through Strath Taieri, the river is already a seasoned traveller. Behind is the hot dry Maniototo Plain; ahead lie two plains and three substantial gorges. The gorges are Hyde, Taieri (Pukerangi to Outram Glen) and Lower Taieri, which cuts through the coastal chain of hills behind Henley, the final barrier before the sea. As the gull flies, the Taieri's headwaters in the Lammermoor Range are little more than 40km from the sea. But rivers and gulls do not have much in common. This river meanders. The Rock and Pillar Range blocks a more direct access to the sea, forcing the river to journey north through the Maniototo until it can find a way around the end of the range at Kokonga. From here it takes a reciprocal course south down the eastern side of the range. By the time it reaches Taieri Mouth, 15km south of Brighton, the river has clocked up 318km. That makes it New Zealand's third longest river. Only the Waikato and Clutha Rivers are longer.

The Taieri drains 5,650 sq km of Otago – about 18 percent of the region. Almost a quarter of the catchment is

> By the time it reaches Kokonga, the city's north-west boundary, for the run south through Strath Taieri, the river is already a seasoned traveller. Behind is the hot dry Maniototo Plain; ahead lie two plains and three substantial gorges.

Left: *Features of the Taieri. Bottom to top: Bulrush or Raupo, flax-lined wetlands, Grey ducks, Taieri Gorge Railway, New Zealand falcon or Karearea.*

Neville Peat

Right: *A newly described species* Olearia fimbriata *tree daisy in Taieri Gorge. This bush is adjacent to the railway line.*

The Taieri 99

over 900m above sea level. The lower end of the Taieri Plain, though, is close to sea level – a few areas are below – and here the river becomes sluggish. A flood protection scheme channels it, anticipating heavy rainfall in the hinterland and a consequent muddy torrent. There is a major flood every few years. Farming and the river have an uneasy relationship on the lower Taieri Plain, which was once an extensive swamp.

Dunedin's largest lakes – Mahinerangi, Loganburn Reservoir, Waipori and Waihola – form part of the catchment. The last two are basically natural; Mahinerangi is a product of a hydro-electric scheme on the Waipori River, and the Loganburn Reservoir feeds a power station and irrigation scheme on the Maniototo, where rainfall is under 500mm a year.

Taieri Mouth is the end of the line for the river, which discharges more or less directly to sea. Not for this river a wallow in an estuary.

The Taieri is tidal for about 15km. Spring tides push as far as Otokia and Lake Waihola. The river's Maori name – more properly, Taiari – refers to a particular tide. Early Maori knew well the link between the tide and phases of the moon and they had names for each phase and degree of tide. They named the river Taiari after the tide on the moon's eleventh night.

> James K. Baxter captured something of the river's life when he wrote in his 1961 poem, 'At Taieri Mouth':
>
> *Flax-pods unload their pollen*
> *Above the steel-bright cauldron*
>
> *Of Taieri, the old water-dragon*
> *Sliding out from a stone gullet*

Below: *Taieri River headwaters high up in the Lammermoor Range.*

Neville Peat

The secret life of Galaxiids

Galaxiids are native freshwater fish widely distributed in New Zealand, including the Chatham Islands and the subantarctic islands. They occupy most freshwater habitats, including swamps, lakes, rivers and mountain streams. Their ancestry goes back tens of millions of years to the break-up of the southern supercontinent of Gondwana.

The best-known Galaxiids form the whitebait catch in spring, chiefly Inaka *Galaxias maculatus*, the adults of which inhabit swamps and low-lying backwaters. Four other species – Koaro *G. brevipinnis*, Banded Kokopu *G. fasciatus*, and the rarer Giant Kokopu *G. argenteus* and Short-jawed Kokopu *G. postvectis* – make up the whitebait catch. The juveniles of these species, after spawning in estuarine areas and washing seaward, live at sea for a few months before returning to the rivers to grow into adults. All species except Short-jawed are found in the Dunedin area.

Other Galaxiid species do not migrate. They remain in their chosen niche the year round. A distinguishing feature of the Galaxiids is their lack of scales. Few people ever see these native fish as adults because of their effective camouflage, their shyness (Kokopu especially) and their choice of bush-clad and forested backwaters as habitat. Except for Giant Kokopu, which can grow to an impressive 58cm in length, they tend to be much smaller than introduced trout, with whom they are now forced to share their habitats.

The Taieri and its tributaries are home to both migratory and non-migratory species of Galaxiid. There are four non-migratory species, reaching lengths of up to 15cm. Only one has been formally described – *Galaxias anomalus*, which lives in lower Maniototo tributaries of the Taieri, notably Kye Burn. It is slender-bodied and variable in colour – grey, brown or olive green. A new species, commonly golden or brown, is found in the Nenthorn area and upper Taieri. There are two other undescribed species. One inhabits Totara Creek on Rough Ridge (Maniototo), the other, identified in a 1995 study, occurs between Stony Creek (Lammermoor area) in the west and Whare Creek, a Silver Stream tributary, in the east. Thus it is a Dunedin endemic. Chestnut brown to black, with bronze markings, it inhabits small streams and pools and is much less shy than Kokopu. Juveniles and adults are often seen swimming about in the day-time.

These Galaxiids have a life span of only a few years - probably just three or four years in the case of *G. anomalus*; seven years for the lower Taieri species. Brown trout and other introduced fish have reduced Galaxiid populations in the Taieri and elsewhere through predation and competition for food. In the Taieri at least, the native fish prosper only when trout are absent or in low numbers.

The lower Taieri galaxiid, Galaxias eldoni, which grows to about 15cm in length and 35g in weight. The structure of its fins is a chief distinguishing characteristic.

Life in the Gorge

River gorges such as the Taieri Gorge have acquired a refuge role for native plants, birds and invertebrate animals by offering steep, rocky and sometimes shaded habitats relatively unaffected by land development.

On either side of the Taieri Gorge the rolling uplands have been extensively modified by farming, but within the gorge significant areas of native shrubland and grassland, and pockets of tall forest, are still to be found.

The schist rock here is estimated to be 150 million years old. The hills are much younger and the river has cut down through them to form the gorge, the longest and most spectacular of the three gorges on the river.

In the lower sections there are stands of podocarp forest featuring Kahikatea and Hall's totara. Kahikatea is very rare in east Otago. Inland, Kanuka and Manuka form dense canopies along the banks. West of Hindon, conditions become distinctly drier and more rocky. The vegetation reduces to scattered shrubland and tussock grassland. On the northern (true left) bank west of Hindon, there is an impressive shrubland community featuring Kohuhu, Broadleaf (Kapuka), Kowhai and various Coprosma species.

Among the indigenous shrubs and small trees in the gorge is a relatively rare *Olearia* or tree daisy. Small-leaved and deciduous, it grows to a height of about 5m and is found in greatest concentrations between the Deep Stream via-

Above: *Rocky stretches of the Taieri Gorge provide habitat for a large black noisy cicada* Amphipsalta strepitans. *As with most cicada species, the males make most of the noise, singing loudly to attract a female. In the case of A. strepitans the song incorporates a rhythmic clapping sound. It is one of three clapping species and is rare in Otago. Taieri Gorge train passengers who disembark briefly at The Reefs should listen out for this cicada on warm days.*

Below: *Female New Zeland falcon at her nest site in the Silver Peaks area. One chick is visible, the other is mantled under the female's wing.*

New Zealand Falcon

New Zealand's only endemic daytime bird of prey, the New Zealand falcon or Kararea *Falco novae-seelandiae*, may be seen anywhere along the Taieri River, although it is rarely observed downstream of the Taieri Plain. The Taieri Gorge is a stronghold. A pair nests every year on bluffs above The Notches.

Superbly quick in the air and agile on the ground, falcons hunt live prey, mainly birds but also lizards, mice and an occasional rabbit. Within territories that may range over 5 sq km they build nests – little more than a scrape – on rock ledges, and they guard them fiercely. Their rapid 'kek-kek-kek-kek' call is used in territorial and courtship displays and when stooping on prey or intruders.

Unlike the larger, slower-moving harriers, which avoid humans, falcons are practically fearless. They will attack people, dogs and tractors in defence of their nest. Females are larger than males. Over autumn and winter, the birds are solitary. Courtship and renewal of the pair bond occurs in July-August, with the male leading the female to the nest site. Two or three chicks are raised. They usually fledge before Christmas or in January and for a few weeks they are taught flying and hunting skills by the parents. A mid-air food pass is one method of instruction.

Being at the top of the food chain, falcons are susceptible to pesticides. They were often shot by farmers in the past for attacking hens and sheep dogs, but have been protected since 1986. Falcons based in the hills around the Mt Allen/Silverstream area occasionally fly over metropolitan Dunedin, and sometimes they go 'window shopping' at the Botanic Gardens aviary, causing the caged birds more than a little anxiety.

---

duct and The Notches. Prominent close to the railway line, it was discovered here in 1993. It is an undescribed species, first recognised in the Upper Pomahaka area, about 100km west of Taieri Gorge, in 1986. A few scattered plants are known elsewhere in Otago and Southland, including a solitary tree on Otago Peninsula.

Below The Notches, between the railway and river, is a stand of Narrow-leaved lacebark *Hoheria angustifolia*. Ferns, including Bracken, are prominent among the native ground-cover plants in the gorge. Flax is also found throughout the gorge.

Gorse and broom are the commonest exotic woody plants, and broom in particular is increasing rapidly to the point of threatening native shrubland. Wilding conifers – *Pinus radiata* and Douglas fir – are beginning to spread. A major threat to native vegetation comes from browsing by wild goats. In the past, clearance of vegetation by burning followed by grazing by farm stock reduced natural values.

There are two small plantations of English oak and Douglas fir next to the railway line between The Notches and Pukerangi. Willows line the river banks through much of the gorge.

In the lower, more vegetated parts of the gorge, there are native bush birds in abundance, including Grey Warbler, Silvereye, South Island Fantail and Bellbird. In smaller numbers are Rifleman, Brown creeper, South Island tomtit, Tui, New Zealand pigeon and Shining cuckoo. Black shags and Southern Black-backed gulls fly back and forth. The shags are breeding on rock ledges in the Hindon area. The gulls have a colony a few hundred metres upstream of the Deep Stream bridge. The native Paradise shelduck is increasing, but it has yet to reach wild geese numbers. Common introduced species are Blackbird, Starling, Yellowhammer and the finches – Chaffinch, Goldfinch and Greenfinch.

New Zealand's two daytime birds of prey – Australasian harrier (hawk) and New Zealand falcon – live in or close to the gorge. The more common harrier is frequently seen working the thermals round the clifftops.

Teucridium

Teucridium parvifolium is a small-leaved divaricating shrub growing to a height of about 2m. It is known from only three sites in Otago, one of them being the Taieri Gorge forest between Outram Glen and Taioma (Trotters Gorge and Gorge Creek near Alexandra are the other two sites). Its leaves are up to 12mm long, and its tiny flowers are pale mauve or white. It is a New Zealand endemic whose main populations are in Canterbury and Marlborough. Its square stems are characteristic.

Above: *The Cabbage tree* Cordyline australis *in flower. One of our most recognisable trees because of its palm-like appearance, it often grows alone in the open, somewhat forlornly.*

Below: *Paradise shelduck pair. The female has the white head.*

Legendary Ti

The Cabbage tree is found through much of the Taieri catchment and probably evolved in New Zealand on forest margins. Known to Maori as ti or ti kouka, cabbage trees were highly important in pre-European times as a food and fibre resource. Stems of young trees were cooked slowly in large ground ovens. Maori undertaking treks into Central Otago relied on it for sustenance. The remains of umu-ti (cabbage tree ovens) are found throughout the Strath Taieri.

Paradise shelduck

Neither duck nor goose but something in between, the Paradise shelduck or Putakitaki *Tadorna variegata* is increasing in number in the Taieri Gorge. Flocks are common along river or stream banks – or in paddocks – on the Strath Taieri and Maniototo Plains. They mate for life and are rarely seen alone. The female, which has a high-pitched alarm call, is easily identified by her white head and chestnut breast, belly and flanks; the male, who has a deep honking call, is essentially black overall. They nest in spring, usually on the ground under logs or tree roots, but also sometimes beside haystacks or buildings, and the eight to 12 eggs are incubated by the female alone. Flightless during the summer moult, they were slaughtered throughout the country last century and in pre-European times, but their numbers are recovering now. In coastal Otago, there is a limited hunting season on the species, which affords a measure of protection. Elsewhere it is a game bird.

Above: *Among the larger mayflies in the Taieri catchment is* Coloburiscus humeralis. *It is commonest in stony tributaries and montane to alpine sections of the Taieri River. Six other mayfly species are known in the Taieri catchment.*

Above: *Of New Zealand's four green stonefly species,* Stenoperla prasina *is common in the Taieri River and its tributaries. The similar but more purple-coloured S.* maclellani *is found in upland parts of the Taieri catchment.*

Aquatic insects

Caddis and mayflies are prominent among the aquatic insects on the Taieri River, but it is in the smaller tributaries and especially the headwater torrents and seepages that insect life becomes diverse and highly specialised.

There are 36 species of caddis inhabiting the Taieri system, including one short-winged species found nowhere else – *Philorheithrus* new species. In the Lee Stream catchment live a local endemic and newly described species *Oeconesus angustus.*

Ponds and lake edges support an array of aquatic insects, including damselflies and dragonflies, backswimmers and waterboatmen and several species of water beetle and midge. Compared to stream insects, these species can tolerate much higher water temperatures as well as less dissolved oxygen. Their habitat generally has luxuriant plant growth, however.

The larval cases of Leptocerid caddis resemble sticks and feed on vegetation and detritus in mainly stagnant waters. Adults are distinctive. They possess long antennae and they fly in a shimmering pattern over the larval habitat. They rest on pond or lakeside vegetation and are active at dusk or in the night.

Among the other orders, New Zealand's only dobsonfly *Archichauliodes diversus* – our largest adult aquatic insect – is numerous in stony montane and lowland parts of the Taieri where the familiar larvae, called toe-biters, are important insect predators. They hide under stones at the water's edge. The large adults, which have wingspans up to 8cm, are conspicuous in flight at night.

Stonefly species are also common in the Taieri system and species diversity increases with altitude up each tributary and towards the river's headwaters. The larvae of all species are found in or close to the water, feeding on plants or detritus. Common in slower-moving and mud-bottomed tributaries as well as in the alpine headwaters is New Zealand's only scorpionfly *Nannochorista philpotti.*

Sedgelands containing flax and *Coprosma propinqua* are rich in bugs, flies and moths, especially if the pedestalled *Carex secta*, which has been called Ballerina sedge, is present. Its skirt of dead leaves and associated litter supports the larvae of many species and provides shelter for adults.

The cosmopolitan moth *Scieropepla typicola* is responsible for the fluffing of Raupo seedheads. Larval workings within the dense seedhead loosens the immature seeds, causing them to pop out involuntarily.

Damselflies such as the blue *Austrolestes colensonis* and red *Xanthocnemis zelandica* are found around stagnant pools. They are slower on the wing and less mobile than dragonflies like *Procordulia smithi* and *P. grayi*, both common here.

WAIHOLA-WAIPORI A wetland mosaic

By any measure – flora, fauna, water resource or landform – the Waihola and Waipori lake and wetland complex is a habitat of exceptional interest to Dunedin, Otago and the country as a whole.

The two lakes and their associated wetlands – a mosaic of streams, channels, backwaters, swamps, deltas and levees – cover about 2,000ha at the southern end of the Taieri Plain. Although 10km inland and screened from the sea by a chain of hills, the system is influenced by the tide via the Taieri River, which pushes saline water into Lake Waihola. Salinity increases in dry spells. Both lakes are shallow (Waihola's mean depth is 1m, Waipori's 0.75m) and both are slowly infilling with silt.

Largely under protection now, the wetlands are a showcase of biological diversity. The largest populations of waterfowl in Otago live here, with no fewer than 11 species represented. In late summer, when moulting is in full swing, bird counts have reached a staggering 20,000. Altogether, 37 bird species breed on the lake shores and throughout the wetlands.

Black swans are the most conspicuous of the waterfowl. Populations of up to 6,000 have been recorded here (see also Chapter 5). Among the ducks, New Zealand shoveler or Kuruwhengi is at home here. Over 3,000 shovelers regularly use the area. Whereas swans are entirely vegetarian, shovelers feed mainly on invertebrates. They are the fastest-flying waterfowl and may move long distances between wetlands to feed and breed.

Among the less common species of waterfowl at Waihola-Waipori are Australasian bittern, Marsh crake and Spotless crake. The crakes, weak-flighted and secretive birds, feed on small crustacea, molluscs, insects and their larvae, and the seeds and tender shoots of various aquatic plants. There have been very few sightings of Spotless crake.

Once uncommon here, New Zealand scaup or Papango is increasing in number at Waipori's Sinclair Wetlands. It is New Zealand's only diving duck. Foot-propelled, it can stay submerged for over half a minute and attain depths of up to 2m. It usually cannot recolonise shallow wetlands where dabbling ducks such as Mallard, Grey and their hybrids prevail; thus its increasing presence here is a tribute to the highly productive nature of this wetland ecosystem.

Waders are also numerous, especially White-faced heron, self-introduced from Australia, whose breeding was first confirmed from Otago in the 1940s. Pied stilt and South Island Pied oystercatcher are reasonably common. Eye-catching Cattle egrets, migrants from Australia, are seen in small flocks in late winter and spring. Occasionally there is a visit from a Little egret, another Aussie migrant, and from

Neville Peat

Above: *Channels, swamps and backwaters linking Lakes Waipori and Waihola (in the distance).*

White herons on lone excursions from the Okarito colony after the breeding season.

The herons are fishing, and the commonest small fish are the Common bully, Smelt and Inaka *Galaxias maculatus*. Black flounder and lamprey inhabit the area, and Yellow-eyed mullet swim in with the tide but do not reside. An ocean-going Kahawai was recorded in Waihola in 1990 during a period of drought and increased salinity. There are good populations of introduced Brown trout and Perch. Green and whistling frogs are common.

For the birdlife, tall grasses, sedges, reeds and shrubs provide habitat for nesting, resting and escape. Dominating the sedgeland is the endemic Purei *Carex secta*, whose droopy-leaved tussocks, mounted on impressive trunks, can reach heights of 3m. It is often associated with Jointed rush, flax, toetoe and shrubs of *Coprosma propinqua*. On the margins of ponds, channels and backwaters are dense stands of Raupo or Bulrush *Typha orientalis*, which requires its roots to be permanently submerged. It reaches heights of 2.5m, and its upright sword-like leaves are strikingly green in summer.

Growing amongst the Raupo and flax close to its southern limit is the Swamp nettle *Urtica linearifolia*, a slender-leaved nettle extending its narrow stems to a height of 2m.

Among the trees that have established on levees and islands, Kanuka reaches 6m in height and is commonly associated with Broadleaf. Underneath, typically, is a shrub layer of *Coprosma crassifolia*, *Corokia cotoneaster* and European broom. Marsh ribbonwood and Cabbage trees are relatively common. There are about 40 tree and shrub species in the wetland.

The Nursery-web spider Dolomedes minor *festoons gorse, broom and other low-growing shrubs with its distinctive white webs in late summer and autumn. The female guards her web and protects the spiderlings as they emerge from the eggsac enclosed within it. Males are almost as big as females and similar in appearance, with a colouring and patterning that makes them readily identifiable. These spiders generally live in paddocks and catch a variety of insects as food. At the Waipori/Waihola wetlands, the spiders are preyed upon by resident fernbirds. The fernbird shakes the shrub to dislodge the female spider as she guards her 'nursery', whereupon the bird swoops in to catch the spider on the ground and carry it off to hungry chicks. Eggsacs are also fed to the fernbird's chicks.*

Fernbird

The Waihola-Waipori wetlands are a favourite haunt of the South Island fernbird *Bowdleria punctata punctata*, whose habitat has been much reduced by the drainage of swamps since European settlement. The fernbird, weakly flighted and nesting close to the ground, is also vulnerable to attack from stoats, ferrets and wild cats. A member of the warbler family and about the size of New Zealand pipit, it will fly for no more than about 100m at a stretch across dense sedgeland/shrubland vegetation. Its tailfeathers are spine-like and often frayed, and the tail tends to droop in flight. It builds its nest in sedges and rushes, and the young, numbering two to four, are fed craneflies, moths, grubs and caterpillars. The Waihola-Waipori wetlands support a breeding population of some 250 pairs, making this site nationally important. The only other large Otago population is at Lake Tuakitoto near Kaitangata. The picture shows fernbird with nestlings in *Carex secta*.

Threats to the wetland

Dynamic and productive, the Waihola-Waipori wetlands may appear resilient, but they do face serious threats in the long run.

Siltation. The lakes and backwaters are infilling gradually with silt, which is carried in by the river, especially during floods. Die-off of Raupo in places is symptomatic of this process. Since European settlement, the system has lost about 800ha to farm development.

Weeds. The crack willow *Salix fragilis*, introduced from Europe, is spreading through the system, accelerating the reclamation. If allowed to spread, European broom will also threaten native shrublands.

Eutrophication. Run-off from surrounding farmland and dairy shed effluent (an estimated one million litres a day of waste water) is boosting nutrient supply to the point where algal blooms, which upset the natural food web by depleting oxygen in the water, are not uncommon. During the 1980s there were seven such blooms. The Otago Regional Council is monitoring water quality, with particular reference to nutrient levels, pH, turbidity and dissolved oxygen levels.

Rod Morris

Pukeko

Related to the endangered flightless Takahe and somewhat like it in colouring, Pukeko *Porphyrio melanotus* is a characteristic bird of the Waihola-Waipori wetlands. The size of a small hen, it can fly and dive but does neither very well. They are highly social birds, sometimes sharing nests. Fighting, done mostly with feet rather than the robust bill, is not uncommon to settle disputes about the pecking order. They move about the swamps and adjacent land in groups, feeding mainly on seeds, shoots and roots but also on small fish, birds or carrion. Flesh forms a large part of the diet of chicks, of which there are usually three to six. Food is often eaten from a raised foot, parrot-like.

Above: *A pair of Pukeko. One adult is preening the other.*

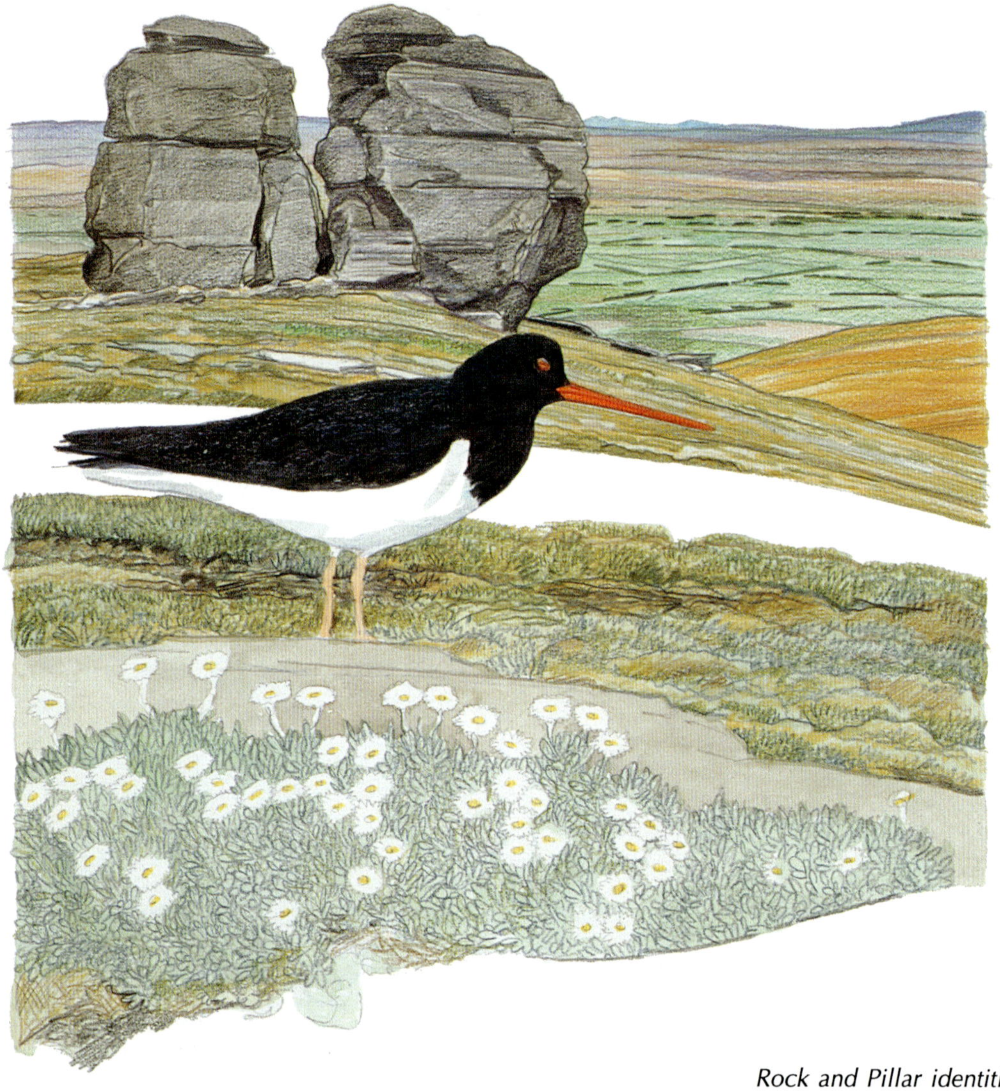

Chris Gaskin

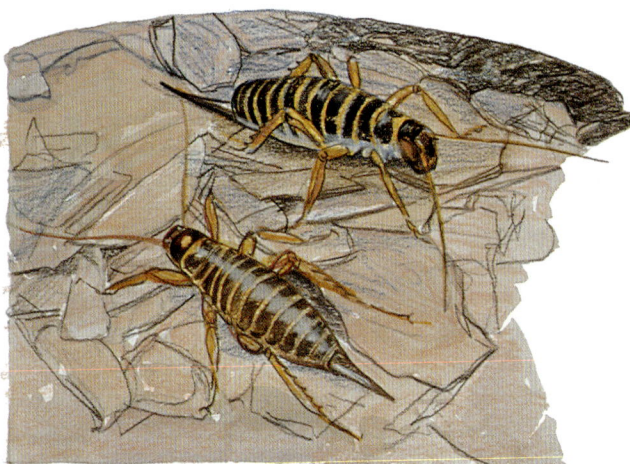

Rock and Pillar identities. Top to bottom: Schist tor overlooking Strath Taieri, cushionfield, South Island Pied oystercatcher in Celmisia viscosa *meadows, local endemic daisy* Celmisia haastii *var.* tomentosa, *female mountain weta* Hemideina maori.

Chapter 9   RANGE ROVING
Rock and Pillar, Lammermoor, Maungatua

Inland, the limits of Dunedin City are alpine, spacious and singularly devoid of human contrivances except for an occasional hut or fenceline. They are the tops of the Rock and Pillar (reaching 1,450m), Lammermoor (1,159m) and Maungatua (895m) Ranges. Snow-laden in winter months and often well into spring, the summit crests and plateaux experience a climate that puts plant and animal life to the test.

The Rock and Pillar Range summit plateau – 23km long and up to 6km wide – has the most severe climate. The mean air temperature is just above freezing and winds buffet the place the year round, averaging close to 30kph. The yellow-brown soils are moist, leached and acidic. Plants need to be tough, well rooted and low-growing. Their growing season is just five months long. Conditions on the Rock and Pillar Range tops are only slightly less severe than on the high ranges to the west, in the heart of Central Otago.

Whereas the Rock and Pillar summit crest contains mainly cushion vegetation and stony or rocky ground, the tops of the Lammermoor and Maungatua Ranges are cov-

Winter scene: Snow coats the Rock and Pillar Range to the valley floor in this mid-winter view from Taieri Ridge.

Neville Peat

ered by a mixture of tall tussock grassland, shrubland and cushionfield. However forbidding the climate may seem compared to conditions near sea level, the alpine zone of Dunedin is species-rich when it comes to plants and invertebrate life.

New Zealand has an extraordinary array of alpine plant species, and for its area there is more diversity than in most other mountainous parts of the world, especially in the Southern Hemisphere. The species lists for Rock and Pillar, Lammermoor and Maungatua contribute to that alpine emphasis in the New Zealand flora. Among the Rock and Pillar plants are four that are found nowhere else.

On the Rock and Pillar, Lammermoor and Maungatua Ranges, the herbfield and cushionfield communities harbour over 150 species – a diversity that the most luxuriant lowland forest cannot match. Snowbanks add a special dimension – and challenge – to alpine flora. On the one hand, snowbanks bury vegetated areas for months on end; on the other, they act as drip-feed water supplies that last into summer months – mountain-top oases. Rock and Pillar Range, being the highest, has the best-developed cushionfield and snowbanks of the three ranges.

Matching a diverse assemblage of plant species on the three ranges is a superb insect fauna. On the Lammermoor Range alone, there are 547 insect species in 13 orders – an outstanding count by New Zealand standards for an alpine area. Some species are endemic to the range. Almost all

Mountain-top Torea

Among the many ironies in nature is the presence of the South Island Pied oystercatcher *Haematopus ostralegus finschi*, a bird commonly associated with ocean beaches and estuaries, on the range tops over summer. Known to Maori as Torea, it breeds inland – on farmland, riverbeds and alpine cushionfield or fellfield. The migration inland occurs from late July, although some non-breeders remain on the coast the year round.

Torea breed from about three years of age and usually pair for life. There are two or three eggs to a clutch and the chicks take five weeks to fledge. Over winter most birds move north, as far as Northland. Invertebrate animals are the bulk of their diet. With long bills, they probe for shellfish at the coast and worms and insect larvae in the mountains. Their calls ('hu-eep' or 'kleep', repeated) are distinctive and, on a still day in the alpine zone, somewhat startling to the visitor. Plump-breasted, they were a popular game bird last century. They are fully protected.

Below: *Herbfield near the summit of the Rock and Pillar Range in early summer, with the 'Pillar' in the background. Snow patches persist above shrubland at the head of the Six-Mile catchment.*

Neville Peat

are native. Introduced species have barely penetrated the alpine zone. The Lammermoor Range and the uplands connecting it with the Rock and Pillar appear to be a sort of insect nerve centre.

Typically for alpine regions, these insects are often larger, hairier and more brightly coloured than their lowland relatives. In addition, many are flightless (or sometimes the female is brachypterous) when kindred species are normally flighted. Diurnal activity is another feature of these alpine invertebrates. Perhaps their habitats are too cool at night; perhaps they are bolder in daylight hours because bird or reptile predators are few in number. Whatever the reasons, the fact remains that an array of strikingly colourful and surprisingly large insects greets the explorer of snow tussock and cushionfield. Despite their wind-swept and rigorous nature climatically, these mountain tops have a sizeable moth fauna.

The short growing season for plants affects insects. Their life cycles are often protracted. It may take several seasons of feeding for larvae to attain sufficient size for metamorphosis to adulthood to take place. This means some years are considerably better than others for viewing alpine insect fauna.

> **Other birds**
> The range tops have a limited avifauna. Besides Torea, two other coastal birds are regularly seen – Southern Black-backed gull (Karoro) and Banded dotterel (Tuturiwhatu). Both breed in the mountains. New Zealand pipit (Pihoihoi) is relatively common and more often seen on the ground than in the air, running daintily or pausing to bob its tail. Australasian harrier (Kahu) overfly the summit crests on patrol for food, and most of the Rock and Pillar, Lammermoor and Maungatua alpine zone will be claimed as territory by pairs of New Zealand falcon (Karearea).

Grasslands of the Rock and Pillar summit plateau, looking northeast across the Maniototo to Mt Ida (1,692m), which is the highest point in the Taieri catchment.

LAND OF TORS

The summit crest of the Rock and Pillar Range is a land of tors and strangely patterned earth.

The tors are sometimes clustered, sometimes standing alone, intact or in various stages of collapse. Survivors of millions of years of erosion, they are the most resistant bits of bedrock schist, rich in quartz. The loess and sediments that buried them, and the mica that helped form the bedrock, have long since been carried away.

The pillars are perhaps the most intriguing, their upright, sheer-sided form a product of vertical jointing. They inspire colourful names, these outcrops – The Castle, Stonehenge, The Window. Indeed, the whole range is named for them. Then there are the blocks that have split and toppled or lie tantalisingly balanced. Large plates of rock dislodged from the tors sometimes turn into 'ploughing' rocks that leave a furrow as they inch down a leeward slope, assisted by the frequent freeze-thaw activity of the weather and the extra water accumulated snow can provide during the extended spring melt.

On gentle or moderate slopes, the ground can take on a waved pattern of crest and furrow, rather like a recently ploughed paddock. These 'soil stripes' are caused by the differential movement of soil and gravels induced by frost and subsequent thawing. When soil freezes it expands, and it moves again on thawing. 'Soil hummocks', another distinctive pattern, are usually found on flatter terrain.

Solifluction terraces occur when the soil turns to a stiff kind of porridge through frost activity and literally, if slowly, flows downslope across an often wide front at right angles to the slope.

And less than a kilometre north of Summit Rock is an intriguing landscape feature – a tarn that freezes over to create a miniature ice wedge. On its downhill side the ice has bulldozed a neatly rounded bank, a natural weir.

Above: *A three-piece balancing act on the Rock and Pillar summit.*

Above: *Patterned ground near Summit Rock on the Rock and Pillar Range.*

Left: *Miniature ice-wedge tarn: Ice forming on this tarn on the Rock and Pillar Summit has pushed up a rounded bank on the downhill side.*

Rock and Pillar tor – a Sphinx, perchance – and lenticular cloud.

South of Summit Rock on the Rock and Pillar Range there are patches of gravel where the wind has stripped away the soil entirely, giving plants little chance of reclaiming this territory.

WETA Honorary rodents

By far the largest invertebrate on the Rock and Pillar Range is the weta *Hemideina maori*, which grows to a length of about 65mm. Part of the tree weta family, it has adapted to an alpine existence, spending the summer days under slabs of schist and nights out feeding on cushion plants and other insects. Males are easily identified by their bulging armoured head and massive claws; females by the ovipositor protruding from their rear ends, through which they lay eggs. Males often guard a harem of females.

In winter and spring the habitat of the wetas is invariably buried under snow. During these months they experience a kind of hibernation under the rocks. The existence of 'anti-freeze' properties in their blood (more properly, haemolymph) has intrigued scientists. Few animals on earth are known to tolerate sub-freezing temperatures for such long periods.

H. maori is found on other Otago mountain ranges and as far north as the Mount Cook region, but the Rock and Pillar populations grow to the greatest size. Their presence on predator-free islands in Lake Wanaka hints at a once more widespread low-altitude distribution. Their faeces, which collect under rocks, resemble rat droppings. Indeed, in the evolutionary scheme of things, weta occupy a niche filled in other lands by rodents such as mice and rats. The largest weta weigh as much as mice. A large ground weta *Hemiandrus focalis* is also common across the Rock and Pillar and Lammermoor summits. The orange-spotted cockroach *Celatoblatta quinquemaculata* is another prominent insect at high altitude and is often found in the company of the wetas.

Right: Weta harem: A male mountain weta with three females. Their sheltering slab of rock was removed to photograph them and carefully replaced afterwards.

Shrublands

Early morning sun illuminates the rich colour of the shrubland belt well developed on the eastern slopes of the Rock and Pillar Range above the Strath Taieri, with fog on the valley floor concealing Middlemarch. Squeezed between tussock grasslands and the herbfield/cushionfield of the alpine zone, the shrubland attains its greatest diversity and density in the upper reaches of the Six Mile Stream catchment. *Hebe (Leonohebe) odora*, *Dracophyllum* and *Cassinia vauvilliersii* are the most significant species, but no fewer than three Podocarps occur in close proximity – Snow totara *Podocarpus nivalis*, Bog pine *Halocarpus bidwillii* and Mountain Toatoa *Phyllocladus alpinus*. The Coprosma group is represented by *C. ciliata* and *C. cheesemanii*. At lower altitudes on the Rock and Pillar Range, but also to some extent the Lammermoor and Maungatua Ranges, the significant shrub species include Inaka *Dracophyllum longifolium*, Mountain flax *Phormium cookianum* and the tree daisies *Olearia ilicifolia*, *O. arborescens* and *O. nummulariifolia*. On the Rock and Pillar they grade into Broadleaf/Narrow-leaved lacebark forest in the gullies. Three groves of Hall's totara are known along the eastern face of the range. Subfossil totara logs have been found as high as 1,000m and numerous small fragments of wood charcoal are buried in soil to the same elevation. Deforestation probably occurred about the twelfth century as a result of fires lit by Polynesians.

Below: *The Black cicada* Maoricicada clamitans, *pictured here on* Hebe odora, *replaces the common grassland cicada* Kikihia angusta *in alpine areas, but is only locally common. The larvae are long-lived, feeding on the root sap for several years – possibly more than five years. In contrast, the adults live for only a matter of days, probably fewer than 10 days, during which time they focus on reproducing. Whether they succeed depends to a large extent on favourable weather. Males sing to attract a female.*

Below: *Three podocarps. Top to bottom: Mountain toatoa* Phyllocladus alpinus, *Snow totara* Podocarpus nivalis *and (centre bottom) Bog pine* Halocarpus bidwillii. *In the centre is* Coprosma ciliata *and at left bottom*, Gaultheria depressa.

Above: *Rock and Pillar endemic: Celmisia haastii* var. *tomentosa, flowering in a typical location in a snowbank on the eastern face.*

Endemic Plants of the Rock and Pillar Range

Celmisia haastii var. *tomentosa*
Kelleria villosa var. *barbata*
Abrotanella cf. *inconspicua*

Above: *Cushionfield plants on the Rock and Pillar Range. At centre is the carrot relative, the smallest Anisotome,* A. imbricata, *showing its small flowers, with the buttercup* Ranunculus enysii *flanking it and* Raoulia hectorii *also prominent.*

ROCK AND PILLAR ALPINE ZONE
A miniature forest

Alpine conditions occur above about 1,200m on the Rock and Pillar Range, where tundra-like plant life has developed on loess-covered schist (in contrast to the vegetation on Maungatua and Lammermoor tops, which is established on extensive peaty deposits).

What some four-wheel-drive visitors to the Rock and Pillar summit crest might regard as a dwarfed, impoverished layer of vegetation is nothing less – to cockroaches, spiders and other ground invertebrates, that is – than a miniature forest and shrubland abounding in plants of diverse form, texture and colour. This is the world of alpine herbs, cushion plants and prostrate herbs.

A plant that specialises in occupying the highest and most exposed sites is *Dracophyllum muscoides*, the smallest of the 30 Dracophyllums whose species name refers to its moss-like form. It flattens its branches and foliage on often gravelly sites on the summit crests and, like such plants, packs its leaves tightly to minimise damage from wind, frost and dehydration. It is a relative of Inaka, the grass tree of subalpine shrublands and tussock grasslands, and grows much more slowly.

Other important plants of the alpine cushionfield include classic 'cushions' such as *Anisotome imbricata*, which is a member of the carrot family and produces carrot-scented flowers, *Phyllachne colensoi, P. rubra, Raoulia hectori, R. grandiflora, Kelleria childii, Celmisia argentea, Hectorella caespitosa* and a newly described species *Abrotanella patearoa*, a moss-like daisy which is a local endemic. Another plant found only on the Rock and Pillar Range is a silvery-green whipcord variety of the Daphne family, *Kelleria villosa* var. *barbata*. The genus Hebe (Leonohebe) is well represented on the tops by whipcord species such as *H. hectorii* and *H. poppelwellii*, while *H. propinqua* is found sparingly in the shrub zone lower down on the mountain side.

The mountain daisy *Celmisia viscosa* is dominant on the Rock and Pillar tops, yet absent from adjacent Lammermoor and Maungatua. Covering large expanses with its tufted, leafy rosettes, it favours dips and more sheltered locations. Its species name (after 'viscous') refers to its sticky flower stalks. This daisy flowers irregularly, some years hardly at all, with a peak flowering in mid-summer. It is joined by *C. ramulosa*, a needle-leaved species, and *C. brevifolia* on rocky sites, often in association with *Hebe buchananii*.

On the most sheltered sites, usually in snowbanks, is a daisy that is the Rock and Pillar's most notable local endemic – the variety *tomentosa* of *Celmisia haastii*, which is superficially similar to *C. viscosa* but which has lighter, greyish foliage, is more prostrate and is restricted to the latest snowbanks. Another daisy that is common and distinctive on Rock and Pillar snowbank margins is *Celmisia prorepens*, a Central Otago endemic, which has leaves that are broader, a brighter green and less leathery than as those of *C. haastii*. It is often associated in the snowbanks with the fern *Blechnum penna-marina* and the dwarf shrub Patotara *Leucopogon fraseri*, whose orange berries are sweet tasting.

Among the characteristic herbs of the Rock and Pillar alpine zone, and eye-catching because of their flowers, are *Gentiana bellidifolia* (white flowers) and the buttercup *Ranunculus enysii*. The diminutive speargrass *Aciphylla hectorii*

Left: Meadows of *Celmisia viscosa* near clumps of neatly-rounded Hebe odora. The 1994-95 summer was a bumper flowering season for this mountain daisy, whose striking pink tinged buds are shown below.

Above: *The largest beetle in the alpine zone is the Carabid ground beetle* Megadromus bullatus, *which reaches a length of 33mm and has a characteristic green sheen.*

A fearsome predator, it is found as high as 1,100m. Beetles are the most diverse order of New Zealand insects and the Maungatua, Lammermoor and Rock and Pillar tops harbour a wide range. Many are diurnal, including the spectacular weevil *Zenagraphus metallescens*, which has a metallic appearance.

Maungatua is listed as the type locality for 41 beetle species thanks to a detailed survey of the range late last century. A flightless chafer in the genus *Sericospilus* was discovered on the Lammermoor Range in December 1991, crawling over alpine herbfield at night.

is also common amongst the Blue tussock, with dense colonies on the McPhee's Rock end of the range.

Lichens are significant in alpine areas. The white shoestring-like *Thamnolia vermicularis* is abundant in places, also brown *Cetraria islandica* subsp. *antarctica* and blackish *Alectoria nigricans*. Small grasses are also abundant. They include Blue tussock *Poa colensoi*, the world-wide alpine plant *Trisetum spicatum*, and very small plants of *Festuca multinodis* and *Agrostis muelleriana*. A small hooked sedge *Uncinia fuscovaginata* and members of the wood-rush family, *Luzula rufa* and the cushion *L. pumila*, are common.

Isolated small patches and solitary plants of Slim snow tussock *Chionochloa macra* across much of the summit crest suggest this taller tussock was probably much more widespread here in the past and could have been dominant when pastoral farming began in the mid-nineteenth century.

Above: *Floral arrangement:* Celmisia ramulosa, *a needle-leaved daisy, flowering amongst* Dracophyllum muscoides *and the white shoestring lichen* Thamnolia vermicularis *at 1,350m on the Rock and Pillar Range in December.*

Below: *This diurnal species of caddis* Zelolessica meizon *was first collected from 'under stones beside a torrent' on the Rock and Pillar Range (1,280m above sea level) in 1981 by the late John Child. Also discovered by him on the Rock and Pillar are the caddis* Tiphobiosis childi, Periwinkla childi *and* Costachorema hecton, *and a stonefly species* Zelandobius childi. *Aquatic insects are especially abundant in alpine seepages, snow caves over small torrents, and creeks that meander through the many wetlands. A total of 27 caddis, 22 stonefly and five mayfly species have been recorded from the alpine crests and slopes of eastern Otago. Some are flightless and have well-developed legs for running.*

Right: *A cataract at 1,320m near the head of Six Mile Stream, Rock and Pillar Range.*

Below left: *Dunedin endemic. The flightless chafer beetle* Prodontria montis, *often seen in daylight crawling over the alpine cushionfields, is found only on the Rock and Pillar and Lammermoor Ranges. It is 12mm long.*

Below right: *The stonefly* Zelandobius kuscheli, *pictured on moss, lives in streams near the Lammermoor and Maungatua tops – its only known Otago location. It was described from Southland.*

Brent Emerson

Brian Patrick

Summer Solstice Musings – Neville Peat

It's 6.30am on the summit of the Rock and Pillar Range, Dunedin's inland edge, 1,450m above worry level. The solstice sun has been bathing this high ground for an hour or two already, having caught the clouds napping. The schist tors extend shadows for up to 50 metres across the 'tundra', a pale-green skin stretched thin across the cold earth. The ground-hugging plants must rejoice over days such as this, free of snow, frost and penetrating wind chill. True, there is a wind from the prevailing south-west quarter, but it is mild compared to the blizzard-makers that routinely stalk this place. Right now there is no snow at all on the summit crest, although ironically great banks of it lie at lower altitudes on the eastern faces of the range – fuel for mountain streams.

The tors are silent, decaying monuments to an unspeakably long geological history – weathered bedrock exhumed by the elements, the bones of the earth. You feel compelled to inspect them from every side, for there is bound to be an animal shape or something poetically abstract awaiting inspection. In the lee are microclimates – refuges no doubt for some plants that are beyond their normal limits of altitude but which are making the best of a chance translocation, their seed having been blown here or carried by a passing bird or animal. Lichens, less constrained than vascular plants and more practised at pushing frontiers, are more at ease. To lichens, a sheltered rock face is as good as soil.

It is a contemplative place at dawn, and quiet except for the whistle and whip of wind on sharply angled rock. Hardly anything moves on this bleakly beautiful, openly wistful landscape. It's too early for the moths and grasshoppers. They need a higher sun angle on their bodies and perhaps a higher air temperature to start up their solar batteries. On mountains you expect to hear water chuckling, but the summit crest is dry, almost desert-like, and suddenly your mouth is dry, too. The unfamiliar tugs at your senses – new smells, the unimpeded views, the vacant feel of the place. Without trees, distance is ready to play tricks. Is that rock outcrop half a kilometre away – or two or three?

Then a skylark calls from on high. The warbling voice is thrown on the wind – a salute to the sun perhaps, for why else sing so long and eloquently? The bird is invisible. No matter. It's the voice that counts, uplifting, convivial. The mountain is awakening.

An expanse of Celmisia viscosa, *spongy to walk upon, on the summit crest of the range.*

High lights – Brian Patrick

Night has descended, clear and calm, on the Rock and Pillar Range. Among some shrubs near the hut, at 1,200m altitude, I lay out my moth-trapping gear. Nothing too technical. There's a white sheet spread wide, upon which I place an ultraviolet tube connected to a battery. I wear a headlight – like a miner's lamp – and keep the butterfly net handy, ready for the first wave of nocturnal moths. I'm alone. My daughter and her friend are in their bunks. They had hoped to stay up and help, but daylight saving in midsummer has delayed the darkness. It's now 11pm, too late for them. Oddly, daylight saving was first mooted by a man who rather liked moth-hunting, George Hudson.

I stare at the blue light spreading across the sheet, and wait. It is a moment that will always excite me. Every light-trapping session is like a journey of discovery, and almost certainly no one's ever done this before at this spot and at this time of year. It's astounding how much insect life is abroad at night. New records and new species are always possible in a place like this. What will come in first? Invariably, the chafer beetles and porina moths are the first to get airborne.

Soon the moths are in a frenzy around the light. A species new to me flashes into its beam. I lunge at it with the net but it's gone. Patience, I know, pays off, because the light is usually too much for them to resist. The new species returns and is bottled. For night-flying creatures that shy away from moonlight, they seem inordinately fascinated by this light. New research shows their compound eyes are deceived by bright light and that what they're trying to do is actually fly past into the dark spaces beyond. It seems their navigation goes haywire in the process and they end up circling and getting further confused. Most moths are simply recorded as they fly past or are released from the net after identification. The few that are caught I will pin.

Next morning I pin and set almost 50 adults, of which six species are new records for the range and two are new species to science, quite likely never before seen by humans. It's a special experience, light-trapping.

Right: *Marsh marigold* Psychrophila obtusa *flowering on a snowbank, Rock and Pillar Range.*

Alan Mark

LAMMERMOOR Tussock country

In contrast to the Rock and Pillar tors and 'tundra' the Lammermoor tops, being lower, are essentially tussock country.

Narrow-leaved snow tussock *Chionochloa rigida* is dominant all along the 10km-long crest, which is broad and gently sloped and averages 1,100m in altitude. In places the tussocks are densely packed and 2m tall. There are few expanses of *C. rigida* left in Otago that are as extensive and unmodified as the Lammermoor snow tussock grassland. Only around the highest points, such as Lammermoor Trig (1,159m), do extensive areas of open cushionfield and shorter grasses prevail.

Left: *Flowing lines: Lammermoor tussock grassland.*

Above: *Sundew Drosera arcturi, about to flower on a Lammermoor wetland, surrounded by Comb sedge Oreobolus pectinatus. The sticky hairs on the leaves trap insects to assist the plant's nutrition.*

The Lammermoor crest and gullies blend into the Lammerlaw Range, which heads out at right angles to form the head of the Maniototo Valley.

Fires in the past are thought to have induced large areas of Blue tussock, which, at the highest altitudes, is associated with cushionfield vegetation in which the main species are *Phyllachne colensoi, Raoulia hectori, Anisotome imbricata* and *Celmisia laricifolia*. Two Kelleria cushion species are found on the Lammermoor Range – one common on the Main Divide and rare in Central and Eastern Otago (*K. croizatii*) and the other endemic to Central Otago (*Kelleria childii*). The former has recently been found for the first time on the Rock and Pillar Range.

Between the tussocks there is another set of plants, including the whipcord Hebes, *H. subulata* and *H. poppelwellii*, diminutive shrubs of *Hebe odora*, the straggling subshrub *Gaultheria (Pernettya) macrostigma*, the large daisy *Celmisia semicordata*, and the eastern-most plants of *Brachyglottis revoluta*. On the largest and latest Lammermoor snowbank (but not on Rock and Pillar) is *Parahebe trifida*, a high-al-

Right: *A wetland system on peat, similar to many that occur on the Lammermoor Range.*

Right: *Stepped pools near the summit of the Lammermoor Range at an altitude of about 1,100m.*

Below: *Flowering cushion of* Donatia novae-zelandiae, *Lammermoor tops.*

Below: *On a bed of moss on a Lammermoor bog –* Utricularia novae-zelandiae *in flower.*

pine species centred on the Garvie Mountains and Old Man Range. Here, it is often associated with the native marsh marigold *Psychrophila* (*Caltha*) *obtusa* and the upland lily *Astelia linearis*.

Snowbanks are rich and extensive, containing a variety of cushion species, including *Phyllacne rubra*, patches of the daisy *Celmisia prorepens* and the uncommon but highly aromatic glaucous herb in the aniseed family, *Gingidia baxterae*.

Just below the crest of the Lammermoor, where it merges with the Lammerlaw Range, there are a stepped series of pools and fingerbogs that form the ultimate headwaters of the Taieri River. Cushion bogs include such species as comb sedge *Oreobolus pectinatus* and the sundew *Drosera arcturi*. There are broad carpets of the moss *Sphagnum cristatum*. The native dandelion *Taraxacum magellanicum* also occurs on wetter sites.

A considerable area of the Lammermoor tops and arguably the least-modified stands of snow tussock grassland were acquired by Conservation Department in the early 1990s for a reserve following a tenure review of Halwyn Station.

Below: *The female Hepialid moth* Aoraia orientalis *has reduced wings and cannot fly. It emerges in autumn and attracts the attention of the large male moths, which fly excitedly around it – a spectacular daytime event that often occurs at the approach of a southerly front. The larvae of most Hepialids live underground in tunnels and they emerge at night to feed on grasses or mosses. Often called swift moths, they are an ancient group whose adults are non-feeding.*

Above: *Grasslands of Narrow-leaved snow tussock* Chionochloa rigida *surround Loganburn Reservoir on the broad plateau between the Rock and Pillar and Lammermoor/Lammerlaw Ranges. The reservoir was created in 1986 on the site of the Great Moss Swamp following the construction of a dam and control gates for a joint hydro-electric and irrigation scheme. Countless invertebrate communities, including possibly undescribed species, were drowned in the process. A study of three sympatric (living in the same area) skink species in the Great Moss Swamp area in the 1980s led to the description of a new species* Leiolopisma inconspicuum, *a southern New Zealand endemic, and a more widespread sub-species* L. nigriplantare polychroma, *in addition to the already named* L. maccanni. *Each species had a preferred habitat and distinct home range within the grassland community.*

Above: *Matching the patterning of its wetland habitat is the striking diurnal Crambid moth* Orocrambus thymiastes *(pictured on* Celmisia argentea*), which reaches its northern limit on the wetlands of the Lammermoor Range. Some 25 species of Orocrambus – half the number of described species – have been recorded from the alpine zone here.*

Above: *The diurnal Geometrid moth* Arctesthes siris, *endemic to Central Otago mountains, inhabits snowbanks and cushion wetlands, including those of the Rock and Pillar and Lammermoor Ranges. The elegant larvae feed on small-leaved Coprosmas and Plantago.*

Right: *Clever camouflage. The Geometrid moth* Paranotoreas brephosata *is the most widespread of an orange-winged group of moths. They are masters of disguise. Predators are fooled into thinking they are chasing an orange moth, but when the moth settles it covers its orange hindwings and effectively disappears from view.*

Below: *A golden-bearded mountain jumping spider, as yet undescribed and unnamed. These jumping spiders are found on most high mountains of Central Otago, including the Rock and Pillar Range. The female pictured is distinguished from the male by the conspicuous band of golden hairs below its eyes. She lays her eggs inside a silken cocoon beneath a rock. When the young hatch they remain close to the cocoon and spend the winter there, emerging to hunt for food only when the snow melts. These spiders are able to survive for 4 to 5 months under snow.*

Above: *The exquisite Geometrid moth* Asaphodes cinnabari *lives in damp herbfields at the northern end of the Lammermoor Range – one of its few known locations. It is pictured feeding on nectar of* Bulbinella angustifolia *flowers. Adults fly in early summer and the pale-green larvae feed on herbs. Geometrid moths have a triangular wing shape. They tend to be light-bodied, colourfully – often bizarrely – patterned, and active by day. Their larvae are mostly looper caterpillars and the adults behave like butterflies in the sunshine, resting periodically to sunbathe with their wings flattened one moment then slowly waving or folded upright the next.*

There are about 30 diurnal Geometrid moths on the Lammermoor and Rock and Pillar Ranges. Most are fast, elusive fliers but they require hot days to become active. The eight Notoreas species in the community vibrate their wings even when settling on a flower to feed, which presumably ensures they can take evasive action if threatened by a predatory tachnid fly. On tors at the northern end of the Lammermoor Range flies a new species of green-and-black Dichromodes.

Range Roving

MAUNGATUA

Although it is the lowest of the three mountain ranges within the Dunedin region, Maungatua (895m at summit) has an impressive catalogue of natural values, and this is reflected in the number of times it has been cited as a type locality both for plants and for insects.

The tallest of New Zealand's speargrass (Wild Spaniard) species, *Aciphylla scott-thomsonii*, was first described from here. It is at home in the tussock grassland/shrubland environment near the top of the range. Similarly, both *Dracophyllum politum*, which forms low hummocks on the summit, and the whipcord shrub *Hebe* (*Leonohebe*) *propinqua* were first described from Maungatua.

Meadow of *Gentiana bellidifolia* on a finger bog, Lammermoor Range.

Narrow-leaved snow tussock *Chionochloa rigida* is dominant on the summit plateau. It surrounds bogs and tarns and mixes with shrubs of *Hebe odora*, which are prominent on all three ranges. The shrub zone extends down to 650m and includes the ubiquitous Cottonwood *Cassinia vauvilliersii*, Inaka *Dracophyllum longifolium* and mountain flax *Phormium cookianum*. Near the summit trig there are patches of Inaka about 2m tall growing with *Coprosma* cf. *pseudocuneata* – a shrubland, probably climax, that predates European settlement and has been protected by bogs from fire.

Tarns and bogs on the summit plateau support Sphagnum colonies. The Bog pine *Halocarpus bidwillii* is notable among the shrub species, which include the mat-forming *Dracophyllum prostratum*, *Pentachondra pumila* and *Cyathodes pumila*. Bogs and hummocky turf are colonised by such cushion plants as *Donatia novae-zelandiae*, *Oreobolus pectinatus*, *Celmisia argentea* and *Phyllachne colensoi*. Maungatua is the

Above: *A fingerbog at the headwaters of Deep Creek on the Lammermoor Range. Kelleria paludosa dominates on the gully floor, with cushion plants holding the edges.*

Above: *Maungatua cushion bog, dominated by cushion mounds of* Donatia novae-zelandiae, *mosses and lichens.*

Left: *Wetland near the Maungatua summit, dominated by the moss* Sphagnum cristatum, *with the sedge* Carex coriacea *in the foreground.*

only Otago location for the lichen *Cladonia aueri*, which is found also on the Longwood Range in Southland, St Arnaud Range in Nelson and at Stewart Island.

As for the mountain daisies, *Celmisia semicordata* subspecies *aurigans* is relatively common and distinctive in the grassland and shrubland communities, occurring frequently in patches. *Celmisia densiflora* and *C. lyallii* are not nearly as common.

On patches of exposed peat west of the summit trig are old trunks and prostrate branches of Bog pine and Pink pine, silvery with age. Moa gizzard stones are scattered about.

The range has had a history of burning and grazing. Cattle have trampled sensitive bogs in the past. But the picture is improving. The Department of Conservation has progressively acquired upper areas of the range and now controls the bulk of it. Interest in conserving the natural vegetation of Maungatua actually pre-dated the department by many years. Maungatua Scientific Reserve (553ha) was created in 1969 in response to a felt need to protect snow tussock, bog and cushion communities on at least one of the ranges of Otago. Such a reserve was first proposed in 1962. It is now linked with the Maungatua Scenic Reserve (273ha) at the northern end of the range above Woodside, which had an even earlier mooting. It dates from the creation of a recreation reserve in 1889.

Above: *Shrubland near the Maungatua summit crest, featuring Inaka* Dracophyllum longifolium, *the large mountain daisy* Celmisia semicordata *and Narrow-leaved snow tussock* Chionochloa rigida, *which is flowering.*

Above: *An exposure of peat, covered by decayed wood, mostly Bog pine* Halocarpus bidwillii – *a scene typical also of the Lammermoor Range and Swampy Summit. Shrubland was more extensive in the past at these altitudes.*

Range Roving 127

Chris Gaskin

Chapter 10   CARETAKING Conservation imperatives

Penguins have stirred the conservation conscience of New Zealanders in recent times. Yellow-eyed penguins have become a wildlife litmus test of our efforts to protect habitat and control predators – and much of the focus is on Otago Peninsula, a mainland stronghold of the Hoiho.

These penguins have run an agonising gauntlet. Much of their habitat has been cleared away or burnt. Their chicks are vulnerable to attacks from stoats, ferrets, cats and dogs. In dry spells, fire can overwhelm them (as happened at the Forest and Bird reserve at Te Rere on the Catlins coast in February 1995, when a burn-off on an adjacent property jumped the fence and 52 penguins, half the local population, perished). On top of the dangers they face on land, penguins are vulnerable to problems in their marine environment. They can drown in set nets or become fatally entangled in plastic strapping. In the 1989-90 summer the mainland population crashed, probably because of a biotoxin present in their food supply.

In response to the Hoiho's plight, the Yellow-eyed Penguin Trust, Forest and Bird and other organisations, not the least, the Department of Conservation, have made the penguin a conservation symbol nationally, and Dunedin is the focus for much of this effort – fundraising, education, revegetation, population monitoring, predator trapping. More than anything, the plight of the Hoiho has emphasised the link between the wellbeing of a species and the condition of its habitat – basic ecology.

Conservation is not a case of throwing a fence around an area in the hope of keeping the plant and animal life within it intact forever. Nature is dynamic, thus conservation has to do with avoiding or buffering sudden change, while letting nature take its course. It has to do with keep-

Left: *Conservation targets. Top to bottom: Otago skink on schist outcrop near speargrass* Aciphylla subflabellata, *Hooker's sea lion suckling pup, Yellow-eyed penguin diving.*

Ken Mason

Right: *Young face of conservation. Kiwi Conservation Club members erect a fence on Quarantine Island as part of a revegetation project on the island.*

ing introduced animal pests and weeds under control, and ensuring that a representative range of natural ecosystems is set aside as reserves.

Not surprisingly, the larger biota capture much of the attention and caretaking, especially birds. Smaller, more cryptic fauna, and low-profile plant species, tend to get overlooked – and sometimes it is too late.

Species diversity in the Dunedin region – let alone the rest of the country – is so great that some insects and plants are disappearing before our eyes. Take moths as an example of local extinctions. Of the total of 834 species recorded in Dunedin, some 34 appear to have disappeared. Thirteen are Geometrid moths, the most notable of which is the orange-coloured *Xanthorhoe bulbulata*. It is gone from Dunedin because its sole larval host, the native cress *Ischnocarpus novae-zelandiae*, has disappeared through grazing by stock. The cress and its moth were both once plentiful over eastern and central areas of the South Island (the Queenstown area is a last main refuge for the cress).

Similarly, coastal Pimelea species are increasingly rare. The sand daphne *Pimelea arenaria* disappeared from Warrington Beach as late as 1985, together with a moth *Ericodesma aerodana* whose larvae tie the leaves of the plant. A plant highly palatable to stock, *Gingidia montana*, which was once plentiful, is now found only where stock cannot reach it. Refuges include the rocky bluffs of Mopanui and Mt Watkin (see page 93).

Native fish, until recent times, have been overlooked as a conservation concern. Like birds and invertebrates, they have suffered through loss of habitat and competition with (or predation by) introduced species. As can be seen in the Taieri River system, galaxiids have tended to lose out in competition with introduced Brown trout. New research into the conservation status of galaxiids is pointing out the need to restrict the spread of trout. There is also a need to create reserves that target the conservation of galaxiids. Sev-

> **Firewood plunder**
> Manuka and Kanuka firewood is still for sale in Dunedin – a reflection of the low esteem in which these two native trees are held. Yet the stands of Kanuka and Manuka in the Silver Stream area and on the slopes of Mt Cargill and Swampy Summit are natural assets, valued as seral woodlands on the way to becoming podocarp/broadleaved forest. Their destruction interrupts the natural revegetation process and removes habitat for insects and insectivorous birds.

Yellow admiral butterflies flocking on Escallonia flowers. The Escallonia tree E. bifida *introduced from South America, is related to New Zealand's Marbleleaf* Carpodetus serratus. *Prudent backyard planting of native and introduced species can help conserve native wildlife.*

Above: *Rocks to the rescue. Extensive ploughing of tussock grasslands has reduced habitat for upland native flora and fauna, but refuges still exist in the rock outcrops.*

eral upland streams, or portions of them, have potential as reserves and an opportunity exists under tenure reviews of pastoral leasehold land for such reserves to be created. For freshwater fish, habitat is not confined to in-stream values; habitat includes the vegetation on the banks, which shades the water and supports insect populations that help feed the fish. Trampling of riparian strips by cattle damages this vegetation and collapses the banks.

Clearly, agriculture and forestry have transformed natural habitats across the board, but the impacts of introduced plants and animals spread far beyond the fencelines and fire breaks. Possums and feral pigs and goats are capable of massive damage unless controlled, and gorse and broom, however decorative their yellow flowers on hillsides, pose major threats to natural vegetation.

Wild pigs range through much of Dunedin's upland and alpine areas. They come as close to the metropolitan areas as the lower slopes of Flagstaff, where their distinctive and sometimes extensive rootings may be seen. They are partial to the tap-roots of speargrass, which belong to the carrot family of plants. Recreational hunting helps keep them contained, but the damage they have done on the Rock and Pillar summit crest is of major concern because of the fragility of the herbfields and cushionfields.

Goats, many of them farm escapees or their descendants, have threatened native shrublands, grasslands and regenerating areas in the Taieri Gorge, Maungatua Range and the Mt Allen-Silver Peaks area. The Department of Conservation is systematically trying to keep the mobs under control. A technique used successfully in the Lower Taieri Gorge involves the placement of a radio transmitter on a goat captured live and released to return to its companions. Shooters, helicopter-borne or on foot, come back later to locate the 'Judas goat' and destroy the mob with which it is running. Deer are present in the forests of the Waipori catchment and sometimes graze on the Maungatua tops. Again, recreational hunting is helping to control numbers.

Not only has Maungatua had more than its fair share of introduced fauna, but it has also attracted considerable weed problems. Migrating slowly upwards, gorse and European broom are threatening the protected areas on the upper slopes. A spray programme by DOC has checked the uppermost infestations.

In some areas, notably Taieri Gorge, European broom is eclipsing gorse as the No. 1 problem plant. Spanish heath *Erica lusitanica* is a threat to snow tussock grasslands in the Silver Peaks and adjacent areas, and nearer the coast, Darwin's barberry *Berberis darwinii* is invading shrublands around Otago Harbour. It is easily distinguished by its racemes of yellow-orange flowers, which resemble tiny daffodils, and its blue berries.

Now that the term 'ecosystem' has achieved a measure of popularity and even won statutory recognition, conservationists can more easily argue for the protection not only of a particular native animal or plant but also for the ecosystem to which it belongs. This ecosystem approach to conservation quickened with the advent in the mid-1980s of the Government's Protected Natural Areas Programme, now managed by DOC. PNA surveys are conducted across ecological districts, a recent one being completed for the Waipori Ecological District, which covers south-west areas of Dunedin. These PNA surveys invariably recommend areas for protection. Interest tends to focus on upland or high-country runs where opportunities can arise to achieve formal protection – or agreements regarding conservative stocking rates and land use – through a process of tenure review or sale.

Large blocks of upland and alpine areas are now coming under Department of Conservation control as a result of tenure review, and the new Conservation Management Strategy, released as a draft in April 1995, proposes a series of conservation parks of 10,000ha or more across several Central Otago ranges. The Lammermoor area, with about 7,500ha already protected, appears to be on the way to

A Burning Issue
The long-held high-country farming practice of burning expanses of tussock to encourage palatable and nutritious new growth and clear the way for introduced pasture species, when combined with grazing, has markedly reduced the extent, density and quality of tall tussock grasslands.

The practice is increasingly challenged by scientists and conservationists as unsustainable. Tussock grassland degradation is most obvious when farmers burn areas too frequently and graze them too soon after the burn. Soil erosion and a reduction in the quality and quantity of water yield may also affect upland areas suffering from excessive burning and grazing. Soil nutrient levels may be boosted for the first two years after burning, which enhances tussock growth, but soil quality declines in the long-term. Some scientists have described the latter-day condition of high-country tussock grasslands as an ecosystem in the process of collapsing.

To reverse the decline, the Otago Regional Council, which authorises burning permits, must adopt criteria for tussock fires that will conserve the remaining stands of Narrow-leaved snow tussock and Red (Copper) tussock. Such criteria might require burn-offs to be spaced at intervals of 15 to 20 years and post-burn grazing to be delayed for two years. The high altitude grasslands of Slim snow tussock *Chionochloa macra* above 1,200m are too vulnerable and should not be burnt at all.

achieving conservation park status. On the Lammermoor's southern slopes is a 1,000ha reserve whose name stands as a landmark of tussock grassland conservation in Otago – Nardoo. Nardoo reserve was created in 1979 following a vigorous debate between a group of nine local and university scientists, led by Dr Alan Mark, and farm development interests. The scientists wanted to preserve a catchment with an altitudinal sequence of native snow tussock but an unsympathetic Land Settlement Board opposed the idea, and in the end decided the lower slopes should be developed as farmland. Fortunately, the upper slopes were protected. They include relic stands of Silver beech forest that support small populations of Jewelled gecko.

Nardoo and Maungatua were among the first reserves on high country tussocklands. In those days the argument was over whether there should be any reserves at all; in the 1990s, as a result of a mounting conservation ethic and the rationale provided by the Protected Natural Areas Programme, tenure review and the nation's new commitment to biodiversity, the network of protected lands in Otago, and especially the high country, is increasing steadily.

Ecosystems inadequately represented in the Dunedin region include montane grasslands and shrublands (as on Taieri Ridge and the Nenthorn area), and snowbanks, low-alpine shrublands and fellfield on the Rock and Pillar and Lammermoor Ranges. In addition, there is a pressing need for more reserves in coastal areas – the saltmarshes of Karitane, for example, and dunelands.

A burn-off on the Rock and Pillar Range that got out of control and threatened the Rock and Pillar Scenic Reserve.

John McMecking

New frontier

The sea is a new frontier for conservation. Whereas the protection of terrestrial values goes without saying today, the idea of protecting a comparable ratio (say, 10 to 15 percent) of coastal waters is still not fully accepted by those with an exploitative interest in the sea.

The exploitative view regards the sea as a bottomless resource, ever able to provide for the needs of humanity, and too large to be polluted or modified in any substantial way. The modern conservation view, solidly behind the concept of marine reserves, holds that coastal marine fauna and flora not only deserve to be protected for their intrinsic values, but also because they and their ecosystems are being radically modified by fishing and/or pollution.

The idea of marine reserves has taken a long time to catch on. Only a handful are in place around the New Zealand coastline. Proposals moving towards Ministerial approval include Nugget Point on the Catlins coast, poised to become the first marine reserve in Otago or anywhere along the South Island east coast. It is surely only a matter of time before a marine reserve is established in Dunedin coastal waters, somewhere between Waikouaiti and Taieri Mouth, for it is a coastline dripping with interest.

The PR challenge of sea lions

Hooker's sea lions are a formidable public relations challenge, now that their numbers are increasing on Otago Peninsula beaches at a time when visitor numbers are also increasing. Unlike fur seals, they are not intimidated by people and usually remain indifferent. But if approached too closely or harassed, they may charge. On flat, hard sand they run as fast as people.

As numbers increase, albeit slowly, so will contact with people. In a bizarre incident at St Clair in 1993, a young male sea lion crossed the road and camped in a resident's backyard for a couple of nights. It had to be chased away by Department of Conservation staff. Most people come across sea lions on beaches, however, and DOC continues to issue warnings to people to stay at least 10m away from hauled-out animals.

Many marine anglers and commercial fishers feel threatened by sea lions, which they regard as competitors for fish. In the Catlins, sea lions have been shot. On Otago Peninsula, fur seals have also been killed, despite their full protection under the law. People are going to have to get used to the idea of sharing the coast with these marine mammals. Whales are marine mammals, too, but few people now would think of shooting them.

Above: *The rugged coast around Sandfly Bay, with Gull Rocks in the foreground, has been suggested as the site of Dunedin's first marine reserve. In the background is Sandymount. All the coastal land here is managed by the Department of Conservation.*

BIBLIOGRAPHY

Allen, R B: 1994. *Native Plants of Dunedin and its Environs.* Otago Heritage Books, Dunedin.
Allen, R B: 1978. *Scenic Reserves of Otago Land District.* Biological Survey of Reserves Report No. 4. Department of Lands and Survey, Wellington.
Allen, R B & Johnson, P N: 1982. *Vegetation of the Dunedin Town Belt.* Botany Division, DSIR, Dunedin.
Allibone, R M & Townsend, C R: 1995. *Galaxiids of the Taieri River: identification, ecology and conservation status.* University of Otago Zoology Department report for the Department of Conservation.
Barrett, B I P & Patrick, B H: 1987. Insects of Snow Tussock Grassland on the East Otago Plateau. *New Zealand Entomologist,* Vol 10: 69-98.
Beever, J; Allison, K W & Child, J: 1992. *The Mosses of New Zealand.* University of Otago Press, Dunedin.
Bishop, G & Hamel, A: 1993. *From Sea To Silver Peaks.* McIndoe, Dunedin.
Brownsey, P J & Smith-Dodsworth, J C: 1989. *New Zealand Ferns & Allied Plants.* Bateman, Auckland.
Campbell, J D: 1985. Casuarinaceae, Fagaceae and Other Plant Megafossils from Kaikorai Leaf Beds (Miocene), Kaikorai Valley, Dunedin, New Zealand. *New Zealand Journal of Botany,* Vol: 311-320.
Carter, J: 1994. *Waipori Ecological District.* A Survey Report for the Protected Natural Areas Programme. Department of Conservation, Dunedin.
Cockayne, L: 1911. *Report on the Dune-Areas of New Zealand.* Department of Lands, Wellington.
Cook, E: 1984. *The Small World in the Heart of Plants.* Hodder & Stoughton, Auckland.
Dalrymple, H K: 1937. *Orchid Hunting in Otago, New Zealand.* Coull Somerville Wilkie Ltd, Dunedin.
Department of Conservation: 1993. *Lakes Waipori and Waihola Wetland – A National Resource Inventory.* Department of Conservation, Dunedin.
Dickinson, K J M; Mark, A F & Lee, W G: 1992. Long-term Monitoring of Non-forest Communities for Biological Conservation. *New Zealand Journal of Botany,* Vol. 30: 163-179.
Dugdale, J S: 1988. *Fauna of New Zealand No. 14.* Lepidoptera-annotated Catalogue, and Keys to Family Group Taxa. DSIR, Auckland.
Dugdale, J S: 1994. *Fauna of New Zealand. Hepialidae (Insecta: Lepidoptera), No. 30.* Manaaki Whenua Press, Lincoln.
Emerson B C & Barratt B I P: In press, 1995. Descriptions of seven new species of the genus *Prodontria* (Coleoptera: Scarabacidae: Melolonthinae) within a phylogenetic framework for the genera *Prodontria* and *Odontria.*
Foord, M: 1990. *The New Zealand Descriptive Animal Dictionary.* The Author, Dunedin.
Fahey, D B: 1986. Weathering pit development in the Central Otago mountains of Southern New Zealand. *Arctic and Alpine Research* Vol 18, No 3: 337-348.
Fordyce, R E & Jones, C M: 1990. Penguin History and New Fossil Material from New Zealand. In *Penguin Biology.* Academic Press, San Diego.
Forster, R & L M: 1970. *New Zealand Spiders an Introduction.* Collins, Auckland.
Forster, R & Forster, L M: 1970. *Small Land Animals of New Zealand.* John McIndoe, Dunedin.
Fraser, J: 1991. *Distribution, Abundance and Selection of Refuge Sites by the Alpine Weta,* Hemideina maori *on the Rock and Pillar Range.* University of Otago, Zoology Department, Dunedin.
Forsyth, J & Coates, G: 1989. *The Dunedin Volcano.* New Zealand Geological Survey, Lower Hutt.
Galloway, D J: 1985. *Flora of New Zealand. Lichens.* Government Printer, Wellington.
Gaskin, C: 1989. *A Walk To The Beach.* Heinemann Reed, Auckland.
Gaskin, C: 1985. *Remote the Land's Heart.* John McIndoe, Dunedin.
Gaskin, C & Peat, N: 1991. *The World of Albatrosses.* Hodder & Stoughton, Auckland.
Gaskin, C & Peat, N: 1991. *The World of Penguins.* Hodder & Stoughton, Auckland.
Gibbs, G W: 1980. *New Zealand Butterflies.* Collins, Auckland.
Given, D R: 1981. *Rare and Endangered Plants of New Zealand.* Reed, Auckland.

Goulstone, J F: 1991. *Landsnails from Dunedin and South-east Otago.* Report to Department of Conservation, Dunedin. 22 pp.

Hamilton, S A: 1991. *The role of Sex Ratio, Spatial Distribution and Head Size in the Mating System of the Rock and Pillar Weta* Hemideina maori. University of Otago, Wildlife Management Report No. 17. Otago University, Dunedin. 33 pp.

Hardy, P F: 1982. *Pastoral Lands Assessment Report. Rock and Pillar Range, Otago.* Department of Lands and Survey, Dunedin.

Heads, M J: 1990. A Revision of the Genera *Kelleria* and *Drapetes* (Thymelaeaceae). *Australian Systematic Botany,* Vol. 3: 595-652.

Heads, M J: 1992. Taxonomic Notes on the *Hebe* Complex (Scophulariaceae) in the New Zealand Mountains. *Candollea,* Vol 47(2): 583-595.

Holdsworth, D K & Mark, A F: 1990. Water and Nutrient Input:Output Budgets: Effects of Plant Cover at Seven Sites in Upland Snow Tussock Grasslands of Eastern and Central Otago, New Zealand. *Journal of Royal Society of New Zealand,* Vol. 20(1): 1-24.

Johnson, P N: 1982. *Forest and Scrub Vegetation on Otago Peninsula.* Botany Division, DSIR.

Johnson, P N: 1992. *The Sand Dune and Beach Vegetation Inventory of New Zealand, Vol. II, South Island and Stewart Island.* DSIR Land Resources, Christchurch.

Johnson, P & Brooke, P: 1989. *Wetland Plants in New Zealand.* DSIR field Guide.

Johnson, P N: 1992. *Otago Peninsula Vascular Plant Flora.* Landcare Research, Dunedin.

Lalas, C & McConkey, S: 1994. *A Survey Method for Estimating the Population Size of Hooker's Sea lions at Otago.* Department of Conservation, Dunedin.

Lee, W G; Fenner, M & Duncan, R P: 1993. Pattern of Natural Regeneration of Narrow-leaved Snow Tussock *Chionochloa rigida* ssp. *rigida* in Central Otago, New Zealand. *New Zealand Journal of Botany,* Vol. 31: 117-125.

Lough, T J; Wilson, J B; Mark, A F & Evans, A C: 1987. Succession in a New Zealand Alpine Community: A Markovian Model. *Vegetatio* Vol. 71: 129-138.

McFarlane, A G & Cowie, B: 1981. Descriptions of New Species and Notes on Some Genera of New Zealand Trichoptera. *Records of the Canterbury Museum,* Vol. 9(91): 353-385.

McKellar I C: 1990. *Geology of the South-west Dunedin Urban Area.* New Zealand Geological Survey, Lower Hutt.

McLellan, I D: 1993. *Fauna of New Zealand. Antarctoperlinae (Insecta: Plecoptera), No. 27.* Manaaki Whenua Press, Lincoln.

Mark, A F: 1994. Effects of burning and Grazing on Sustainable Utilisation of Upland Snow Tussock (*Chionochloa* spp.) Rangelands for Pastoralism in South Island, New Zealand. *Australian Journal of Botany,* Vol. 42: 149-161.

Mark, A F: 1994. Patterned Ground Activity in a Southern New Zealand High Alpine Cushionfield. *Arctic and Alpine Research,* Vol. 26(3): 270-280.

Mark, A F & Adams, N M: 1983 (revised edition). *New Zealand Alpine Plants.* A H & A W Reed.

Mark, A F & Bliss L C: 1970. The High-Alpine Vegetation of Central Otago, New Zealand. *New Zealand Journal of Botany* 8: 381-451

Martin, W M: 1924 (Reprinted 1962). *Native Plants of Dunedin and Surrounding District.* Otago Daily Times, Dunedin.

Mason, B: 1988. *Outdoor Recreation in Otago. A Recreation Plan, Vol I.* Central Otago's Block Mountains. Federated Mountain Clubs of New Zealand, Wellington.

Mason, B: 1989. *Outdoor Recreation in Otago. A Recreation Plan, Vol. II.* Silverpeaks and Otago's Alps. Federated Mountain Clubs of New Zealand, Wellington.

Moore, P J: 1995. *Yellow-eyed Penguin Foraging Study, South-eastern New Zealand, 1991-93.* Department of Conservation, Science and Research Series No. 83, Wellington.

Morris, R & Forsyth, J: 1986. *Almost An Island – Guide to Otago Peninsula.* John McIndoe, Dunedin.

Mortimer, N: 1993. *Geology of the Otago Schist and Adjacent Rocks.* 1:500 000. Map No. 7. Institute of Geological and Nuclear Sciences Ltd, Lower Hutt.

Murray, D L; Jackson, R M & Fahey, B D: 1990. Tall Tussocks and Water Yield. In *Southern Landscapes.* Edited by G Kearsley & B Fitzharris. University of Otago, Dunedin.

Naylor, M: 1954. A Checklist of the Marine Algae of the Dunedin District. *Transactions and Proceedings of the Royal Society of New Zealand,* Vol. 82(3): 645-663.

New Zealand Geological Survey: 1969. *The W N Benson Map of Dunedin*. New Zealand Geological Survey, Lower Hutt.

Oliver, W R B: 1937. The Tertiary Flora of the Kaikorai Valley, Otago, New Zealand. *Transactions and Proceedings of the Royal Society of New Zealand*, Vol. 66(3): 284-311.

Oliver, W R B: 1956. The Genus Aciphylla. *Transactions of the Royal Society of New Zealand*, Vol. 84(1): 1-18.

Patrick, B H: 1984. Lammermoor-Lammerlaw – A Tussockland National Reserve in Eastern Otago? *Forest & Bird*, Vol. 15(4): 7.

Patrick, B H: 1989. *The Lepidoptera of Central Otago Saltpans*. Department of Conservation, Dunedin.

Patrick, B H: 1990. Occurrence of an Upland Grassland Moth in a Coastal Saltmarsh in Otago. *Journal of Royal Society of New Zealand*, Vol 20(3): 305-307.

Patrick, B H: 1991. Description of a New Species of Crambidae:Crambinae (Lepidoptera) from New Zealand. *New Zealand Journal of Zoology*, Vol. 18: 357-362.

Patrick, B H: 1994a. *The Importance of Invertebrate Biodiversity*. An Otago Conservancy Review. Conservation Advisory Science Notes No. 53. Department of Conservation, Wellington.

Patrick, B H: 1994b. A Reassessment of the Status of *Olinga fumosa* Wise 1958 (Trichoptera: Conoesucidae) as a Valid Species. *New Zealand Entomologist*, Vol. 17: 78-80.

Patrick, B H & Green, K J: 1991. Notes on *Agrotis innominata* Hudson (Noctuidae: Noctuinae). *New Zealand Entomologist*, Vol. 14: 32-36.

Patrick, B H; Barratt, B I P; Ward, J B & McLellan, I: 1993. *Insects of Waipori Ecological District*. Department of Conservation, Dunedin. Miscellaneous Series No. 11.

Patterson G B & Daugherty C H: 1990. Four new species and one new subspecies of skinks, genus *Leiolopisma* (Reptilia: Lacertilia: Scincidae) from New Zealand. *Journal of the Royal Society of New Zealand*, Vol. 20 (1): 65-84.

Paviour-Smith, K: 1956. The Biotic Community of a Salt Meadow in New Zealand. *Transactions of the Royal Society*, Vol. 83(3): 525-554.

Peat, N: 1992. *The Falcon and the Lark*. John McIndoe, Dunedin.

Probert K & Westerskov K: 1981. *The Seas Around New Zealand*. Reed, Wellington.

Richdale, L E: 1957. *A Population Study of Penguins*. Oxford University Press.

Simpson, G & Scott-Thomson, J: 1938. The Dunedin Sub-district of the South Otago Botanical District. *Transactions of the Royal Society of New Zealand*, Vol. 67: 430-442.

Shaw, T: 1994. *Population Size, Distribution, Home Range and Translocation of the Jewelled Gecko,* Naultinus gemmeus, *at the Every Scientific Reserve, Otago Peninsula*. University of Otago Wildlife Management Report No.56.

St George, I: 1992. *Wild Orchids in the Far South of New Zealand*. Wellington.

Talbot, J M; Mark, A F & Wilson, J B: 1992. Vegetation-environment relations in snowbanks on the Rock and Pillar Range, Central Otago, New Zealand. *New Zealand Journal of Botany* Vol 30: 271-301.

Thomson, G M: 1890. Botany of Neighbourhood. In *Picturesque Dunedin* edited by A Bathgate.

Turbott, E G (Convenor): 1990. *Checklist of the Birds of New Zealand*. Ornithological Society of NZ Third Edition.

Ward, G and Munro, C M: 1989. *Otago II Biological Survey of Reserves Series No. 20*. Department of Conservation, Wellington.

Wardle, P & Mark, A F: 1956. Vegetation and Climate in the Dunedin District. *Transactions of the Royal Society of New Zealand*, Vol. 84(1): 33-44.

Webb, C J; Sykes, W R & Garnock-Jones, P J: 1988. *Flora of New Zealand, Vol. 4*. Botany Division, DSIR, Christchurch.

Whitaker, A H: 1988. *A Survey of the Lizards of the Rock and Pillar Range Area*. Otago Giant Skink Survey No. 8. Department of Conservation, Dunedin.

White, M E: 1986. *The Greening of Gondwana*. Reed, Sydney.

Wilson, H: 1982. *Stewart Island Plants*. Field Guide Publication, Christchurch.

Wilson, C M & Given, D R: 1989. *Threatened Plants of New Zealand*. DSIR Field Guide.

Winterbourn, M J & Gregson, K L D: 1989. Guide to the Aquatic Insects of New Zealand. *Bulletin of the Entomological Society of New Zealand* No. 9, Auckland.

INDEX

Figures in italics refer to illustrations.

Abbotsford 20
Abrotanella patearoa 9, *117*
Acaena pallida 43
    novae-zelandiae 43
Acanthisitta chloris chloris see Rifleman
Aciphylla aurea 86, 82
    glaucescens 86, 92
    hectorii 118
    scott-thomsonii 86, *86*, 126
    subflabellata 86, 92, *94*, 95, *128*
    see also speargrass
Agrostis innominata 56
    muelleriana 118
Akeake 39
Akiraho 55
albatross 24, 25, 28-9
    Northern Royal 27
    Royal 7, *22*, 25, *26*, 27-31, *27*, *28*
    Wandering 28, 29
Allans Beach *23*, 41
Allocharis 9
alpine species 111-28
Alsolemia cresswellii 9, 77
Ammophila arenaria see Marram grass
Amphipsalta strepitans 102
Anemone tenuicaulis 89
anise, Climbing 52
aniseed see *Gingidia* spp.
Anisotome aromatica 91
    imbricata 117, *117*, 122
Anthus novaeseelandiae see pipit
Aoraia 7, 70
    orientalis *124*
    rufivena 76, *76*
Apium prostratum 55, 94
Aporostylis bifolia 84
Apteryoperla 90
Arachaeocete 10
Arachnocampa luminosa 74
Aramoana 7, 12, 14, 59, 60, 61-6, 68
Archaeocete 10
Archichauliodes diversus 105
Arctesthes catapyrrha 43, *69*
    siris *124*
Arctocephalus forsteri see seal, NZ fur
Argyrophenga antipodum 90
    janitae 82, *90*
Aristotelia serrata 38
Asaphodes cinnabari *125*
    obarata 81
Astelia 72, *73*, 74
    fragrans 89
    linearis *123*
    nervosa 89
Austrocidaria parora 81
Austrolestes colensonis 105
Austrovenus stutchburyi see cockle, NZ

Bachelor's button 62, 69
barberry, Darwin 132
basalt 11, 13, 16, 93
bat, NZ Long-tailed 78
beech 16, 81
    Black 80
    Hard 80
    Mountain 80
    Red 75, 77, 80
    Silver 16, 55, 68, 70, 71, *79*, 80, 81, 89, 133
beetles, endemic 9
    Ground 90, *90*, 118
    Longhorn 90, *91*
Bellbird 53, 75, 81, 103
Beriberis darwinii 130
bidibid, Sand 43
bindweed, native 52
bittern, Australasian 106
Black Head *11*, 12, 86
Blechnum capense 82, *87*, 89
    discolor 74
    penna-marina 118
Blueskin Bay 49, 56, 65, 68, 69
bog plants 126-7
Boulder Beach Conservation Area 40
Bowdleria punctata see Fernbird
Brachyglottis repanda 77
    revoluta 122
    rotundifolia 39
    sciadophila 39, *40*
bracken, native 55
Brighton *18*, 19
Broadleaf 38, 52, 71, 72, 76, 87, 93, *93*, 102, 108, 116
broom, European 56, 132
    native see *Carmichaelia* spp.
Bulbinella angustifolia 89, *125*
bully, Common 108
bulrush see Raupo
buttercup see *Ranunculus* spp.
butterfly, Copper 44, 53, 90
    Red admiral 6, *22*, 25, 44, 53
    Tussock 53, *83*, 90
    White 43
    Yellow admiral *130*

Cabbage tree 54, 104, *104*, 108
caddis *8*, 9, *43*, 45, 105, *119*
    Peninsula 45, *45*
Caladenia lyallii 84
Caltha obtusa see *Psychrophila obtusa*
Calystegia soldanella 56
    tuguriorum 52
Caples terrane 18, *18*, 19
Carex apressa 43
    coriacea *125*
    secta 105, 108, *108*

Cargill, Mt (Kapukataumahaka) 11, 14, 71, 72, 83, 91, 95, 130
Carmichaelia virgata 37
Carpodetus serratus 38, 71, *77*, 130
Cassinia vauvilliersii 87, *87*, 116, 126
Casuarina 16
Caversham Valley 7, 9, 78
cedar, NZ 73, 83, *84*, 88
Celama parvitis 38
Celatoblatta quinquemaculata 115
celery, native 55, 94
Celmisia 88
    argentea *117*, *124*, 126
    brevifolia 117
    densiflora *127*
    gracilenta 89
    haastii 9, *110*, 118
    haastii var. *tomentosa* *110*, 117, *117*
    hookeri 84
    laricifolia *122*
    lyallii *127*
    prorepens 118, *123*
    ramulosa 117, *119*
    semicordata 122, 127, *127*
    viscosa *110*, 117, *118*
Cephalissa siria 92
Cetraria islandica subsp. *antarctica* 118
Chafer 62
    flightless 118, *119*
Chalinolobus tuberculatus 78
Charixena iridoxa 72
Charles, Mt 7, *23*, 24
Chenopodium ambiguum 94, 95
Chenopodium conspicua 85
Chionochloa macra 118, 130
    rigida 85, 122, *124*, *127*
    rubra cuprea 68, 85, *85*
cicada, 7, 90, 102, 116
Circus approximans see harrier, Australasian
Cladonia aueri *127*
Clematis vitalba 77
cockle, NZ 63-4, 67
cockroach, orange-spotted 115
Colobanthus muelleri 42
Coloburiscus humeralis 105
Conical Hill 20
Conocephalus bilineatus 95
convolvulus, sand 56
Cook's scurvy grass 43, 51, 55
coprosma 16, 40, *52*, 69, 95, 96, 102, 124
    Sand 56, *56*
Coprosma acerosa 56, *56*
    areolata 38
    cheesemanii 88
    ciliata 88, *116*

Index 139

crassifolia 38, 39, 108
foetidissima 41, 73
grandiflora 77
propinqua 38, *46*, 46, *96*, 105, 108
pseudocuneata 126
repens see Taupata
rotundifolia 38
rubra 38
rugosa 88
virescens 93
Cortaderia richardii 85
Cordyline australis see Cabbage tree
Coriaia plumosa 88
  sarmentosa 88
cormorants *see* shag
Corokia 95
  cotoneaster 37, 39, 108
Costachorema hecton 119
Cottonwood *see Cassinia vauvilliersii*
Cotula coronopifolia 62, 69
crabs 37, 64, 67, *68*, 69
crake, Marsh 106
  Spotless 106
crane-fly 9
Crassula moschata 51
Crater, The 21
creeper, Brown 80, 81, 103
cress, native 43, 130
cricket, native Black 95
cuckoo, Longtailed 80
  Shining 81, 103
Cupressus macrocarpa 24, 40
Cyathodes empetrifolia 88, *88*
  juniperina 38-9
  pumila 126
Cygnus atratus see swan, Black

Dacrycarpus dacrydioides see
  Kahikatea
Dacrydium cupressinum see Rimu
daisy, Cape Saunders rock *41*, 42
  Climbing *see Brachyglottis sciadophila*
  Tree 39, 88, *99*, 102, 116 *see also Celmisia* spp.
damselfly 105
dandelion, native 123
Daphnes, native 42, 88, 130
Dasyuris transaurea 91
Deborah Bay 60
Declana egregia 72, *73*
deer 132
Delogenes limodoxa 43
Desmoschoenus spiralis 40
Diasemia grammalis 43
Dichromodes 123
Diomedea bulleri 28
  cauta 28
  epomophora see albatross, Royal
Disphyma australe 43
dobsonfly 105
Dolomedes minor 43, *108*
dolphin, Bottlenose 34

Common 34
Dusky 34
Donatia novae-zelandiae 123, 126, *126*
Dotterel, banded *58*, 64
Douglas fir 71, 88, 103
Dracophyllum longifolium 42, 87, 116, 126, *127*
  muscoides 117, *119*
  politum 126
  prostratum 126
  uniflorum 88
dragonfly 105
Drosera arcturi 122, 123
Drymoanthus flavum 40
duck, Grey 63, *98*, 106
  Mallard 63, 94, 106
Durvillaea antarctica 67
  willana 67

Ectopatria aspera 61
eelgrass 63
egret, Cattle 106
  Little 106
Elaeocarpus hookerianus see Pokaka
Elderberry 40
Elymus tenuis 94
endemic species 9
Erica lusitanica 132
Ericodesma aerodana 130
Escallonia 130
  bifida 131
Eucalyptus regans 68
Eudonia 9
Eudyptula minor see penguin, Blue
Eurythecta leucothrinca 69
Eutorna symmorpha 69
Every Scientific Reserve 46
extinct marine species *10*

falcon, NZ 6, 84, 94, 97, *98*, *102*, 103, 113
fantail, South Is. 81, 103
fault lines 13
  Alpine fault 19
fern, Crown 74
  Hound's tongue 55
  shield *75*, *81*
Fernbird 7, 62, 108
ferret 28, 53, 97
Festuca multinodis 118
Flagstaff (Whakari) 6, 7, 71, 72, 79, 83-9, *85*, 131
flax, Mountain 87, 116, 126
  NZ 43, *53*, 55, 62, 69, 103, 108
flounder 67, 108
Forget-me-not 42, 94
fossils 10, *12*, 13, 16, 17, 20, 32-3, 71, 116
Foulden Hill 20, 21
Frasers Gully 13,16, *17*
frog, green 108
  whistling 108

Fuchsia, excorticata 92 *see also* Kotukutuku
  perscandens 40, *92*

Galaxias anomalus 101
  argenteus 101
  brevipinnis 101
  fasciatus 101
  maculatus 101, 108
  postvectis 101
Galaxiid fish 9, 16, *17*, 68, 101, *101*, 130-1
Gaultheria depressa 88, *116*
  macrostigma 88, *88*, 122
gecko, Common 51, 54
  Jewelled 25, 46, *46*, 133
Gelophaula 9
Gentiana bellidifolia 118, *126*
geology 11-21
Gingidia baxterae 123
  montana 92, 130
Glasswort 61, *61*
Glenfalloch 24
glow worm 74
Glyphipterix 9
Goat (Rangiriri) Is. 49, 52-3, 54
goats 131-32
godwit, Eastern Bar-tailed *58*, 64, 67
gorse 36, 103, 132
grasshopper 90, *91*
Grass tree 42, 87, 88
Green (Okaihae) Is. 6, *49*, 50, 56, 67
Griselinia littoralis see Broadleaf
groundsel, Shore 43
gull, Redbilled 26, 54, 64, *64*
  Southern Black-backed 26, 50, *52*, 53 64, 81, 94, 103, 113
Gunnera monoica 75
Gymobathra 9

Haematopus ostralegus finschi see
  oystercatcher, South Is. Pied
  unicolor see oystercatcher, Variable
Hakeke *see Olearia ilicifolia*
Halocarpus bidwillii see pine, Bog
Harakeke *see* flax, NZ
Harbour Cone (Hereweka) 22, 24, 38, *39*, *53*
harebell 89
harrier, Australasian 67, *84*, 94, 97, 103, 113
harvestmen 9
Haumakoroa 41
Hawksbury Lagoon 65, 66
heath, Spanish 132
Hebe buchananii 117
  elliptica 6, 39, 43, *50*, 51
  hectorii 117
  odora 88, 90, 91, 116, *116*, *118*, 122, 126
  poppelwellii 117, 122

propinqua 117, 126
salicifolia 39
subulata 122
Hectorella caespitosa 117
Helichrysum aggregatum 37, *38*
 intermedium var. *tumidum* 9, *41*, 42
Hemiandrus focalis 115
Hemideina maori 110, 115, *115*
Hemigrapsus edwardsii 68
Hemiphaga novaeseelandiae see pigeon, NZ
Hereweka *see* Harbour Cone
heron, White 64, 108
 White-faced 64, 94, 106
Hikaroroa *see* Watkin, Mt
Hoheria angustifolia 38, 77, 103
 populnea see Lacebark
Hoiho *see* penguin, Yellow-eyed
Hoiho Trust 32; *see also* Yellow-eyed Penguin Trust
Hoopers Inlet 23, 65, 67-8
Hoplodactylus maculatus see gecko, Common
Horopito *see* Pepper tree
Hupiro *see Coprosma foetidissima*
Hydriomena arida 75

ibis, Glossy 67
Iceplant 43, *53*
Ichneutica 9
Ida, Mt *113*
Ileostylus micranthus 40, *52*, 75
Inaka (grass tree) 42, 87, 100, 126, *127*
Inaka (whitebait) 101, 108
Insects 90, 112-13, 118
 aquatic 105, 119
 see also under species name
Ischnocarpus novae-zelandiae 130
Isolepis marginata 69

Jasmine, native 40, 52, 55
Jointed rush 62, 69, 108

Kahawai 108
Kahikatea 75, 102
Kahu *see* harrier
Kaikawaka *see* cedar, NZ
Kaikorai Estuary 49, 51, *63*, 65
Kaka 71
Kamahi 72
Kamautaurua Is. *see* Quarantine Is.
Kanuka 6, 38, 39, 76, 79, 80, 81, 102, 108, 130
Kapuka *see* Broadleaf
Kapukataumahaka *see* Cargill, Mt
Kareao *see* Supplejack
Karearea *see* falcon, NZ
Karitane 133
Karoro *see* gull, Southern Black-backed
Katipo 57, *57*

katydid 95
Kawaupaka *see* shag, Little
Kelleria childii 117, 122
 croizatii 122
 dieffenbachii 89
 laxa 89
 paludosa 126
 villosa var. *barbata* 9, 117
kelp, bladder 62, *66*
 bull *35*, 67, *67*
Kikihia angusta 90, 116
kingfisher, NZ 67, 68
Kiokio fern *82*, *87*, 89
Kiwaia 9
Knightiella splachnirima 95
Koaro 101
Kohuhu 38, 52, 54, 93, 101
Kokopu 101
Koromiko *see Hebe* spp.
Korora *see* penguin, Blue
Korthalsella lindsayi 40
Kotare *see* kingfisher, NZ
Kotuku-ngutupapa *see* spoonbill, Royal
Kotukutuku 38, 71, *73*, 76
Kowhai *4*, 38, *75*, 102
krill 34, 64
Kuaka *see* godwit, Eastern Bar-tailed
Kukupa *see* pigeon, NZ
Kunzea ericoides see Kanuka
Kuruwhengi *see* shoveler, NZ

Lacebark 75, 77
 Narrow-leaved 38, 77, 103, 116
Lacewing 38, *38*
Lactrodectus katipo 57, *57*
Lammermoor Range 5, 9, 94, 100, 111-13, 115, 116, 118, 119, 122-5, *122*, *123*, 127, 132-3
lamprey 101
lancewood, Fierce 39
Larus dominicanus see gull, Southern Black-backed
 novaehollandiae see gull, Red-billed
Lavatera arborea 51
Lawyer, leafless 40
Leiolopisma chloronoton 54
 grande 96-7, *97*, 98
 inconspicuum 124
 maccanni 124
 nigriplantare polychroma 124
 otagense 96-7, *97*, 98
Leith Saddle 73-4, 83
Leith Valley *4*, 9, 71, 72, 73, 74-5, 78, 81
Lemonwood *see* Tarata
Leonohebe odora see Hebe odora
Leonohebe propinqua see Hebe propinqua
Lepidium oleraceum 43, 51, 55
Leptocarpus similis 62, 69

Leptospermum scoparium see Manuka
Leucocarbo chalconotus see shag, Stewart Is.
Leucopogon fraseri 43
Libocedrus bidwillii see cedar, NZ
lichens 95, *97*, 118, *119*, 126
Lilaeopsis novae-zelandiae 62, 94
lily *see Astelia* spp.
limestone 11, 18
Limosa lapponica baueri see godwit
Lupin 40
Luzula pumila 118
 rufa 118
Lycaena salustius see butterfly, Copper
Lyperanthus antarcticus 84, *84*

Maakoako 61
Macrocarpa 24, 40
Macrocystis pyrifera 62, *66*
Mahoe 38, 39, 52, 71, 73, 75
Makomako 38
mallow, tree 51
Manatu *see* ribbonwood, Lowland
Manuka 56, 69, 79, 80, 87, 102, 130
Maoricicada clamitans 116
Maori onion *see Bulbinella angustifolia*
Mapou 39, 76
Marbleleaf 38, 71, *77*, 130
marigold, native marsh 123, *127*
Marram grass *22*, 40, 55, 57
Matagouri 6, 95
Matai 28, *70*, 71, 75, 76, 80
Maungatua Range 11, 71, 72, 80, 81, 86, 90, 95, 111-13, 116, 118, 119, 126-8, 132
 Scenic Reserve 127, 133
mayflies 45, 105, *105*, 119
Megadromus bullatus 118
Megadyptes antipodes see penguin, Yellow-eyed
Melicytus alpinus 96
 crassifolius 42
 micranthus 75
 ramiflorus see Mahoe
Mesolamia marmorata 91
Meterana 9
Meterana octans 75
Metrosideros diffusa 40, 52
 excelsa 77
 umbellata 56, 72, 77
Micromus bifasciatus 38, *38*
Microtis unifolia 84
Milk tree 38, 75
Mimulus repens 62
Mingimingi 38
mineral resources 18, 20, 21
Miro 54, 73, 74
Mirounga leonina see seal, Elephant
mistletoe 40, *52*, 75, 77
 broad-leaved 75
 red *70*, 81

Index 141

moa 89, 127
Mohoua novaeseelandiae 80
Mohua 71
Mole, The 14, 26, 43
mollymawk, Buller's 28
   Whitecapped (Shy) 28
Monterey cypress 24, 40
Morova subfasciatus 44
moths *38*, 40, 43, 61, *69*, 72, *73*, 75, 81, 90, *90*, *92*, 95, 105, 113
   Aoraia 7, 70, 76
   crambid 43, *124*
   Diamond-back 43
   endemic 9
   Geometrid 43, 69, 91, 124, *124*, 125, *125*, 130
   hepialid 76, *124*
   micro-casemoth 52, *54*
   Muehlenbeckia 44, *44*
   noctuid 56
   porina 76
   pyralid 43
   Streblus *75*
   Zebra *73*
   Zigzag *72*
   see also under species name
Moturata (Taieri) Is. 55-6, 59
Mountain holly *see Olearia ilicifolia*
Muehlenbeckia australis 38, 44, 90
   complexa 96, 97
   moth 44, *44*
mullet, Yellow-eyed 108
Munida gregaria 64
musk, saltmarsh 62
Muttonbird scrub 39
Muttonbird *see* shearwater, Sooty
Myoporum laetum see Ngaio
Myosotis 9, 94
   pygmaea var. *pygmaea 42*
   rakiura 42
Myrsine australis 39, 76

Nannochorista philpotti 45, *45*, 105
Nardoo Reserve 133
Naultinus gemmeus see gecko, Jewelled
Nenthorn 83, 84, 94, 96, 101, 133
Nertera setulosa 43
nettle, Swamp 108
   Tree *see* Ongaonga
Ngaio 38, 39, 52, 54, 69
Ngiru-ngiru *82*
Nothofagus 16
   fusca 75, 77
   menziesii see beech, silver
Notoreas spp. 125
Nuncia sublaevis 9
Nyctiphanes australis 64

Oeconesus 9, 105
Oioi *see* Jointed rush
Okaihae *see* Green Is.
Okia Flat 38, 41, 43

Old Man's Beard 77
Olearia 95, *99*, 102
   arborescens 39, 88, 116
   avicenniifolia 39
   ilicifolia 41, 116
   nummulariifolia 116
   paniculata 55
Olinga fumosa 8
Ongaonga 22, 39, 44
orchids 40, 84, *84*
Oregus inaequalis 90, *90*
Oreobolus pectinatus 122, 123, 126
Orihou *see* Three-finger
Orocrambus thymiastes 124
Orokonui Inlet 68-9, 81
Otago Harbour *14-15*, 59, 60, 67, 68
Otago Peninsula 7, *7*, 9, 11, 12, *14-15*, 23-46, *47*, 54
Otekiho 41
Ovalipes catharus 68
oystercatcher, South Island Pied 27, 64, 67, 94, 106, *110*, 112
   Variable (Black) *22*, 27, *27*, 50

Pacific Plate 14, 19
Painted Forest 89, *89*
Papango 106
Papanui Inlet 14, 23, 36, 65, 67-8
Parahebe trifida 122
Paranotoreas brephosata 125
Parekareka *see* shag, Spotted
Parsonsia heterophylla see Jasmine, native
Pasiphila charybdis 50
   fumipalpata 50
Pate 76
Patotara 43, 118
Peggy's Hill 24, 41
penguin, Blue 26, 29, 31, *48*, 50
   Erect crested 32
   extinct *10*, 33
   Fiordland crested 32
   fossil *10*, *12*, 13, 33-4
   Rockhopper 32
   Snares crested 32
   Yellow-eyed (Hoiho) 7, *22*, 24, 26, 29, 32-3, *33*, 44, 50, *128*, 129
Pentachrondra pumila 88, *88*, 126
Peppertree 39, *52*, *82*, 83
Peraxilla colensoi 81
Perch 108
Pericoptus truncatus 62
Peripatus 7, 9, *70*
   Caversham 78, *78*
Periwinkla childi 119
Pernettya macrostigma see Gaultheria macrostigma
Petroica australis see robin, South Island
Phalacrocorax melanoleucos see shag, Little
Philanisus plebeius 45, *45*

Philorheithrus 105
Phocarctos hookeri see sea lion, Hooker's
Phormium cookianum 87, 116, 126
   tenax see flax, NZ
Phycomorpha metachrysa 75
Phyllachne colensoi 117, 122, 126
   rubra 117, 123
Phyllocladus alpinus 116, *116*
Phymatosorus diversifolius 55
pigeon, NZ *70*, 72, *74*, 75, 81, 103
pigs 131
Pihoihoi *see* pipit
Pimelea 130
   arenaria 130
   aff. *urvilleana* 42, 88
   oreophila 88
pimpernel, Shore 61
pine, Black *see* Matai
   Bog *116*, 126, 127, *127*
   Pink 89, 127
   White *see* Kahikatea
Pingao 40
Pinus radiata 71, 81, 87, 103
pipi 67
pipipi 80
pipit, NZ 91, *91*, 113
Pittosporum eugenioides 71, *74*, 75
   tenuifolium see Kohuhu
Plagianthus divaricatus see ribbonwood, Saltmarsh
   regius see ribbonwood, Lowland
Plantago 69, 124
Platalea regia see spoonbill, Royal
plover, Spur-winged 67, 94
Poa annua 51
   astonii 43, 54
   cita 42, 55
   colensoi 118
Poaka *see* stilt, Pied
Podocarpus hallii see totara, Hall's
   nivalis 116, *116*
Pohutukawa 55
Pokaka 38, *39*
Polystichum vestitum 81
Porcupine shrub 96, 97
Poroporo 40, 55
Porphyrio melanotus 109
Porrhothele antipodiana 71
possums 53, 131
Pounuiahine Is. *see* White Is.
Prasma sorenseni regalia 9
prion, Fairy 50, 54
Procordulia grayi 105
   smithi 105
Prodontria montis 119
protea 16
Prumnopitys ferruginea see Miro
   taxifolia see Matai
Pseudocoremia lactiflua 69
Pseudoeconesus 9, 43
Pseudopanax colensoi see Three-finger

ferox 39
simplex 41
Pseudowintera colorata see Peppertree
Psychrophila obtusa 123, *127*
Pteridium esculentum 55
Pteronemobius bigelowi 95
Pudding (Titeremoana) Is. 49, *52*
Puffinus griseus see shearwater, Sooty
Pukeko 63, 109, *109*
Pukekura 14, *16*, 25 see also Taiaroa Head
Pukekura Pa *25*
Purakanui 59
Purei see *Carex secta*
Putakitaki see shelduck, Paradise
Putaputaweta see *Carpodetus serratus*
Pyramids, The *11, 23*
Pyrrosia eleagnifolia 40
Pyura pachydermatina 67

Quarantine (Kamautaurua) Is. 49, *52, 53,* 52-4, *129*

Rabbit Is. 49, 56, 69
rabbits 53, 55
Rakiri 14
Rangiora 77
Ranunculus enysii 117, 118
Raoulia 42
   australis 42
   beauverdii 43
   grandiflora 117
   hectori 117, 11, 122
rata, Climbing 40, 52
   Southern 56, 72, 77
rats 28, 53, 97
Raupo 65, 98, 105, 108
Raurekau 77
Reductoderces spp. *54*
Remuremu see *Selliera radicans*
ribbonwood, Lowland 75, 77
   Saltmarsh *61*, 62, 69, 77, 108
Rifleman 38, 39, *80,* 103
Rimu 38, *39,* 73, 76, 80
Ripogonum scandens 38, 54
Rirīrangi Is. see Goat Is.
robin, South Is. 7, *70,* 77, 79
Rock and Pillar Range *5,* 7, 9, 11, *19,* 110, 111, 111-16, *111-15,* 131, *133*
   alpine zone 117-19
   Scenic Reserve 133
rosellas 68
   Eastern 81
Rubus squarrosus 40

Sabatinca quadrijuga 91
Saddle Hill 14
Salix fragilis 109
Samolus repens 61-2

Sandfly Bay Wildlife Refuge 40, 135
sandstone *10, 12*
   Caversham 13, 20, 21
Sandymount 6, 18, 24, 39, 40, 42, 44, 135
   Recreational Reserve 40
   Wildlife Refuge 68
Sarcocornia quinqueflora 61, *61*
Saunders, Cape *23,* 35, *42*
Scandia geniculata 52
scaup, NZ 106
Sceliodes cordalis 40
Schefflera digitata 76
schist 18-19, *18, 19,* 21, 83, 89, 92, 94, 96, 102, *110,* 117, *129*
Schoenoplectus pungens 61, 69
Scieropepla typicola 105
Scleranthus uniflorus 42
Scoparia tuicana 90
Scoriodyta patricki 54
Scorpionfly 45, *45,* 105
Scots pine 54
Scythris nigra 90
seagrass 63, 64, 65
seal, Elephant 34, 36
   Leopard 34
   NZ fur 6, *22,* 24, 34, 35
sea lion 7, 24
   Hooker's 34, *36, 37,* 36-7, *128,* 134
Sea tulip 67
sedge 61, 62, 69, 118, *128*
   Ballerina 105
   Comb 122, 123
   see also *Carex* spp.
Selliera microphylla 94
   radicans 61-2, *62,* 69
Senecio carnosulus 43
Sericospilus 118
shag, Black 103
   Little 25, 30, *48,* 50, *51,* 53
   Spotted 25, 26, 29, *30,* 31, 54
   Stewart Is. 25, 29, 30, *31, 48,* 50, 54
shearwater, Sooty 25, 26, *48,* 50, 55, *55*
shelduck, Paradise 67, 94, 103, *104*
sheoaks 16
Shore Spinach 43
Shoveler , NZ 63
Sigaus australis 91
Silvereye *75,* 81, 103
Silver Peaks 14, 71, 72, 83, 86, 89, 95, *102,* 132
Silver Peaks Scenic Reserve 83
Silver Stream 78, 79, 130
Simplicia laxa 84
Sisters, The 20
skink, Grand 96-7, *97*
   Green 54
   Otago 96-7, *97, 128*
skinks 124

Smelt 108
snails 9, 77
snowberries *88,* 89
   see also *Gaultheria* spp.
Solanum laciniatum 40, 55
   see also *Aciphylla* spp.
Sophora microphylla see Kowhai
Spaniard, Wild 83, *86,* 126
Spartina angelica 62
speargrass 131
   see also *Aciphylla* spp.
Speedwell, coastal see *Hebe elliptica*
Sphagnum cristatum 123, *128*
spider, jumping 125
   Katipo 57, *57*
   Nursery-web 108
   tunnelweb 71
   water 43
spoonbill, Royal 7, *48, 49,* 50, 51, *51,* 64
St Martin Is. see Quarantine Is.
Staphylinid beetles 62
Starling 50
Steinera sorediata 95
Stenoperla maclellani 105
   prasina 105
Sterna striata see tern, Whitefronted
Stictocarbo punctatus see shag, Spotted
Stigmella aigialeia 69
stilt, Pied *58,* 64, 94, 106
Stinkwood see *Coprosma foetidissima*
stoat 28, 53, 97
stoneflies 45, *90,* 105, *105,* 119
Strath Taieri 9, 18, 83, 94, 97, 104, *110*
Streblus heterophyllus 38, 75
Styles Creek Bush 40, 41, 46
Suaeda novae-zelandiae 62
sundew *122,* 123
Supplejack 38, 54
Sutton Lake 94-5, *94, 95*
Swampy Summit 6, 8, 9, 43, 71, 72, 83-90, *85-7,* 95, *127,* 130
swan, Black 64, *65,* 65-6, 94, 106

Tadorna variegata see shelduck, Paradise
Taiaroa Bush 38
Taiaroa Head (Pukekura) 14, *16,* 23-31, *30, 31,* 35, 36
   Nature Reserve 28
Taieri Gorge 7, 102, *102,* 132
Taieri Is. see Moturata Is.
Taieri Plain *8,* 75
Taieri Ridge 19, 20, 83, 133
Taieri (Taiari) River/Mouth 71, 72, 75, 99-110, *100,* 123, 130
Tara see tern, White-fronted
Tarapunga see gull, Red-billed
Tarata 71, *74,* 75
Taratu Formation 21

Taraxacum magellanicum 123
Tauhinu *see Cassinia vauvilliersii*
Taupata 6, 50, 51
Tawhai *see* beech, Silver
tern, White-fronted 26, *53*
Tetragonia trigyna 43
Teucridium parvifolium 103
Thamnolia vermicularis 118, *119*
Thelymitra hatchii 84
   longifolia 84
   venosa 84
Three-finger 72, 73, *82*, 88
Ti, Ti kouka *see* Cabbage tree
Tiphobiosis childi 119
Titeremoana Is. *see* Pudding Is.
Titeremoana Scenic Reserve 55
Titi *see* shearwater, Sooty
Titi-wainui *see* prion, Fairy
Tmesipteris tannensis 74
Tmetolophota purdii 72
Toatoa, mountain 116, *116*
Toetoe 85, 108
Tomtit, South Is. 82, 103
Topshells 64
Torea *see* oystercatcher, South Is.
   Pied
Torea-pango *see* oystercacher,
   Variable
Torlesse terrane 18, *18*, 19
Toroa *see* albatross, Royal
Tortricidae 9
Totara 54, 71, 80
   Hall's 38, *52*, *52*, 69, 73
   Snow *116*
Toutouwai *see* robin, South Is.
Town Belt 76-7
Tree daisy 39, 88, *99*, 102, 116
Tree fuchsia *see* Kotukutuku

Tree nettle 22, 39, 44
Trisetum spicatum 118
trout, Brown 101, 108, 130
Tui 75, 103
Tunnel Beach *12*, 50
Tupeia antarctica 77
Turepo 38, 75
Turpentine shrub 88
turtle 10
tussock 43, 54, 68, 69, 85, *85*, 87-8,
   90, 94, 96, 118, 122-4, 126, 132-3
   see also Poa spp., *Chionochloa* spp.,
   Festuca spp.
Tutu 88
Tuturiwhata *see* dotterel, Banded
Typha orientalis see Raupo

Uncinia fuscovaginata 118
Undaria pinnatifida 62
Urtica ferox see Ongaonga
   incisa 44
   linearifolia 108
Utricularia novae-zelandiae 123

Veronica, NZ *see* Hebe
Victory Beach 36, 37, 43
volcanism 11-13, 14, *14-15*, 16, *16*,
   20-1, 50, 83, 89, 90, 92

Wahlenbergia albomarginata 89
Waikouaiti 60, 65
Waiora 16
Waipori Falls Scenic Reserve 80
Waipori/Waihola 7, 65, 71, *79*, 80-
   1, 100, 106-9, *106-7*, 108, 132
warbler, Grey 53, 80, 81, 103
Watkin (Hikaroroa), Mt 83, 92-3,
   92, *93*, 130

weevil 118
Weinmannia racemosa 72
weta, cave *91*
   ground 115
   mountain 110, 115, *115*
Whakari *see* Flagstaff
whale *10*, 134
whale, Orca (Killer) 34
   Southern right 34, *34*
Wharekakahu Is. 49, *54*
wheatgrass 94
whelks 64
White (Pounuiahine) Is. 49
whitebait 101
Whiteywood *see* Mahoe
willow 103, 109
Wineberry 38
Woodhaugh Gardens 74, 75
Woodside 75, 81, 127

Xanthocnemis zelandica 105
Xanthoparmelia 97
Xanthorhoe bulbulata 130

Yellow-eyed Penguin (Hoiho) Trust
   33, 41, 129
yellow-brown soils 111
yellow-grey earth 16
Yellowhead 71

Zelandobius childi 119
   foxi 45
   kuscheli 119
   uniramus 45
Zelandotipula 9
Zelolessica meizon 119
Zenagraphus metallescens 118
Zostera novazelandica 63, 64, 65

ACKNOWLEDGEMENTS

The authors are especially grateful to the Dr Marjorie Barclay Trust, the Dunedin Branch of the Royal Forest and Bird Protection Society and the Otago Conservancy of the Department of Conservation for their generous support.

Professor Alan Mark provided valuable guidance throughout the project.

Chris Gaskin's series of paintings do much to enhance the book's visual impact. His expertise is gratefully acknowledged.

For their assistance with scientific information, thanks are also extended to Richard Allibone, Dr Barbara Barratt, Associate Professor Doug Campbell, Sally Carson, Professor Doug Coombs, Dr Brent Emerson, Malcolm Foord, Dr Ewan Fordyce, Drs Ray and Lyn Forster, Dr David Galloway, Tony Harris, Dr Peter Johnson, Dr Chris Lalas, Dr Peter McIntosh, Ian McLellan, Dr Nick Mortimer, Christopher Robertson, Dr Richard Sadleir, Dr John Ward, and Dr John Youngson. Thanks also to Otakou Marae for help with Maori names.

The publishers thank the following for the donation of photographs: Department of Conservation, Ray Forster, Brent Emerson, Peter Johnson, Rory Logan, Graeme Loh, John McMecking, Alan Mark, Ken Mason, Brian Patrick and Neville Peat.